6. Enter your class ID code to join a class.

IF YOU HAVE A CLASS CODE FROM YOUR TEACHER

a. Enter your class code and click | Next |

b. Once you have joined a class, you will be able to use the Discussion Board and Email tools.

c. To enter this code later, choose **Join a Class**.

IF YOU DO NOT HAVE A CLASS CODE

a. If you do not have a class ID code, click | Skip |

b. You do not need a class ID code to use *iQ Online*.

c. To enter this code later, choose **Join a Class**.

7. Review registration information and click Log In. Then choose your book. Click **Activities** to begin using *iQ Online*.

IMPORTANT

- After you register, the next time you want to use *iQ Online*, go to www.iQOnlinePractice.com and log in with your email address and password.
- The online content can be used for 12 months from the date you register.
- For help, please contact customer service: eltsupport@oup.com.

WHAT IS iQ ONLINE ?

All new activities provide essential skills **practice** and support.

Vocabulary and Grammar **games** immerse you in the language and provide even more practice.

Authentic, engaging **videos** generate new ideas and opinions on the Unit Question.

Go to the Media Center to download or stream all **student book audio**.

Use the **Discussion Board** to discuss the Unit Question and more.

Email encourages communication with your teacher and classmates.

Automatic grading gives immediate feedback and tracks progress.

Progress Reports show what you have mastered and where you still need more practice.

OXFORD
UNIVERSITY PRESS

198 Madison Avenue
New York, NY 10016 USA

Great Clarendon Street, Oxford, OX2 6DP, United Kingdom

Oxford University Press is a department of the University of Oxford.
It furthers the University's objective of excellence in research, scholarship,
and education by publishing worldwide. Oxford is a registered trade
mark of Oxford University Press in the UK and in certain other countries.

Director, ELT New York: Laura Pearson
Head of Adult, ELT New York: Stephanie Karras
Publisher: Sharon Sargent
Managing Editor: Mariel DeKranis
Development Editor: Eric Zuarino
Executive Art and Design Manager: Maj-Britt Hagsted
Design Project Manager: Debbie Lofaso
Content Production Manager: Julie Armstrong
Senior Production Artist: Elissa Santos
Image Manager: Trisha Masterson
Image Editor: Liaht Ziskind
Production Coordinator: Brad Tucker

ISBN: 978 0 19 481904 6 Student Book 3 with iQ Online pack
ISBN: 978 0 19 481905 3 Student Book 3 as pack component
ISBN: 978 0 19 481802 5 iQ Online student website

Printed in China
This book is printed on paper from certified and well-managed sources.

ACKNOWLEDGEMENTS

*The authors and publisher are grateful to those who have given permission to
reproduce the following extracts and adaptations of copyright material:*

p. 160 from "Happiness Breeds Success ... and Money!" by Sonja
Lyubomirsky, July 18, 2008, http://www.psychologytoday.com. Used by
permission of Sonja Lyubomirsky.

Illustrations by: p. 4 Jing Jing Tsong; p. 28 Bill Smith Group; p. 48 Bill Smith
Group; p. 78 Bill Smith Group; p. 89 Barb Bastian; p. 102 Bill Smith Group;
p. 128 Barb Bastian; p. 152 Barb Bastian; p. 176 Bill Smith Group.

*We would also like to thank the following for permission to reproduce the following
photographs:* Cover: David Pu'u/Corbis; Inside back cover: lvcandy/Getty
Images, Bloom Design/shutterstock; Video Vocabulary (used throughout the
book): Oleksiy Mark / Shutterstock; p. 2/3 MCMULLAN CO/SIPA/Newscom;
p6 Artiga Photo/Corbis UK Ltd.; p. 16 Art Directors & TRIP/Alamy; p. 18
UpperCut/Oxford University Press; p. 26 Ariel Skelley/Blend Images/Cor/
Corbis UK Ltd.; p. 27 Africa Studio/Shutterstock (sweets); p. 27 Wutthichai/
Shutterstock (vitamins); p. 27 Jason Loucas/Getty Images (fest food); p. 30
Jason Loucas/Getty Images; p. 35 Bon Appetit/Alamy (ice cream); p. 35
Steve Cavalier/Alamy (coffee); p. 36 Photodisc/Oxford University Press
(chocolate); p. 36 Photodisc/Oxford University Press (coffee); p. 36 Scott
Karcich/Shutterstock (cheese); p. 41 Stock Connection/Superstock Ltd.; p. 42
Aurelie and Morgan David de Lossy/Getty Images; p. 43 Paul Abbitt/Alamy;
p. 46 luoman/iStockphoto; p. 47 SoFood/Alamy (fondue); p. 47 Tim Hill/
Alamy (paella); p. 48 Stockbyte/Oxford University Press; p. 52/53 Richard
T. Nowitz/Corbis UK Ltd.; p. 56 Tetra Images/Oxford University Press;
p. 61 Rex Features; p. 72 David Madison/Corbis/Oxford University Press;
p. 76 Caro /Alamy; p. 77 SilvaAna/iStockphoto (menu); p. 77 Stacy Walsh
Rosenstock/Alamy (bicycle); p. 78 SeanPavonePhoto/Shutterstock; p. 81
Venus Angel/Shutterstock (pram); p. 81 Timmary/Shutterstock (perfume);
p. 81 Shutterstock/Maksim Kabakou/Oxford University Press (phone);
p. 100/101 Mark Moffett / MINDEN PICTURES/Getty Images; p. 102 Monalyn
Gracia/Corbis UK Ltd.; p. 103 Ariel Skelley/Blend Images/Cor/Corbis UK Ltd.;
p. 111 Stuart Westmorland/Science Fa/Corbis UK Ltd.; p. 122 imagebroker/
Alamy (Pantheon); p. 122 Neus Grandia/Oxford University Press (map);
p. 126 Alistair Berg/Getty Images; p. 126/127 ZING Studio/iStockphoto;
p. 127 Bennyartist/Shutterstock (turbines); p. 127 VLADGRIN /iStockphoto
(illustration); p. 129 HolgerBurmeister/Alamy; p. 134 Moodboard/Corbis
UK Ltd.; p. 137 Subic/Getty Images; p. 140 Huntstock, Inc/Alamy; p. 150/151
Bernd Kohlhas/Corbis UK Ltd.; p. 153 Photodisc/Oxford University Press;
p. 157 Steven S Miric/Superstock Ltd.; p. 159 Simon Jarratt/Corbis UK
Ltd.; p. 160 Dana Patrick/Sonja Lyubomirsky, Ph.D.; p. 165 David Noton
Photography/Alamy; p. 174 Steve Debenport/Getty Images; p. 175 david
pearson/Alamy (medal); p. 175 Marmaduke St. John/Alamy (scoreboard);
p. 176 Photodisc/Oxford University Press (reading); p. 176 Image Source/
Corbis UK Ltd. (runner); p. 176 fStop/Alamy (woman); p. 177 Paul Collis/Alamy;
p. 178 Photodisc/Oxford University Press; p. 180 PCN Photography/Alamy;
p. 182 Moodboard/Corbis UK Ltd.; p. 183 Lebrecht Music and Arts Photo
Library/Alamy.

SHAPING learning TOGETHER

We would like to acknowledge the teachers from all over the world who participated in the development process and review of the Q series.

Special thanks to our Q: Skills for Success Second Edition Topic Advisory Board

Shaker Ali Al-Mohammad, Buraimi University College, Oman; Dr. Asmaa A. Ebrahim, University of Sharjah, U.A.E.; Rachel Batchilder, College of the North Atlantic, Qatar; Anil Bayir, Izmir University, Turkey; Flora Mcvay Bozkurt, Maltepe University, Turkey; Paul Bradley, University of the Thai Chamber of Commerce Bangkok, Thailand; Joan Birrell-Bertrand, University of Manitoba, MB, Canada; Karen E. Caldwell, Zayed University, U.A.E.; Nicole Hammond Carrasquel, University of Central Florida, FL, U.S.; Kevin Countryman, Seneca College of Applied Arts & Technology, ON, Canada; Julie Crocker, Arcadia University, NS, Canada; Marc L. Cummings, Jefferson Community and Technical College, KY, U.S.; Rachel DeSanto, Hillsborough Community College Dale Mabry Campus, FL, U.S.; Nilüfer Ertürkmen, Ege University, Turkey; Sue Fine, Ras Al Khaimah Women's College (HCT), U.A.E.; Amina Al Hashami, Nizwa College of Applied Sciences, Oman; Stephan Johnson, Nagoya Shoka Daigaku, Japan; Sean Kim, Avalon, South Korea; Gregory King, Chubu Daigaku, Japan; Seran Küçük, Maltepe University, Turkey; Jonee De Leon, VUS, Vietnam; Carol Lowther, Palomar College, CA, U.S.; Erin Harris-MacLead, St. Mary's University, NS, Canada; Angela Nagy, Maltepe University, Turkey; Huynh Thi Ai Nguyen, Vietnam; Daniel L. Paller, Kinjo Gakuin University, Japan; Jangyo Parsons, Kookmin University, South Korea; Laila Al Qadhi, Kuwait University, Kuwait; Josh Rosenberger, English Language Institute University of Montana, MT, U.S.; Nancy Schoenfeld, Kuwait University, Kuwait; Jenay Seymour, Hongik University, South Korea; Moon-young Son, South Korea; Matthew Taylor, Kinjo Gakuin Daigaku, Japan; Burcu Tezcan-Unal, Zayed University, U.A.E.; Troy Tucker, Edison State College-Lee Campus, FL, U.S.; Kris Vicca, Feng Chia University, Taichung; Jisook Woo, Incheon University, South Korea; Dunya Yenidunya, Ege University, Turkey

UNITED STATES Mary Ahlman, Coastline Community College, Westminster, CA; Marcarena Aguilar, North Harris College, TX; Rebecca Andrade, California State University North Ridge, CA; Lesley Andrews, Boston University, MA; Deborah Anholt, Lewis and Clark College, OR; Robert Anzelde, Oakton Community College, IL; Arlys Arnold, University of Minnesota, MN; Marcia Arthur, Renton Technical College, WA; Renee Ashmeade, Passaic County Community College, NJ; Anne Bachmann, Clackamas Community College, OR; Lida Baker, UCLA, CA; Ron Balsamo, Santa Rosa Junior College, CA; Lori Barkley, Portland State University, OR; Eileen Barlow, SUNY Albany, NY; Sue Bartch, Cuyahoga Community College, OH; Lora Bates, Oakton High School, VA; Barbara Batra, Nassau County Community College, NY; Nancy Baum, University of Texas at Arlington, TX; Rebecca Beck, Irvine Valley College, CA; Leslie Bennett, UCLA, CA; Linda Berendsen, Oakton Community College, IL; Jennifer Binckes Lee, Howard Community College, MD; Grace Bishop, Houston Community College, TX; Jean W. Bodman, Union County College, NJ; Virginia Bouchard, George Mason University, VA; Kimberley Briesch Sumner, University of Southern California, CA; Kevin Brown, University of California, Irvine, CA; Laura Brown, Glendale Community College, CA; Britta Burton, Mission College, CA; Allison L. Callahan, Harold Washington College, IL; Gabriela Cambiasso, Harold Washington College, IL; Jackie Campbell, Capistrano Unified School District, CA; Adele C. Camus, George Mason University, VA; Laura Chason, Savannah College, GA; Kerry Linder Catana, Language Studies International, NY; An Cheng, Oklahoma State University, OK; Carole Collins, North Hampton Community College, PA; Betty R. Compton, Intercultural Communications College, HI; Pamela Couch, Boston University, MA; Fernanda Crowe, Intrax International Institute, CA; Vicki Curtis, Santa Cruz, CA; Margo Czinski, Washtenaw Community College, MI; David Dahnke, Lone Star College, TX; Gillian M. Dale, CA; L. Dalgish, Concordia College, MN; Christopher Davis, John Jay College, NY; Sherry Davis, Irvine University, CA; Natalia de Cuba, Nassau County Community College, NY; Sonia Delgadillo, Sierra College, CA; Esmeralda Diriye, Cypress College & Cal Poly, CA; Marta O. Dmytrenko-Ahrabian, Wayne State University, MI; Javier Dominguez, Central High School, SC; Jo Ellen Downey-Greer, Lansing Community College, MI; Jennifer Duclos, Boston University, MA; Yvonne Duncan, City College of San Francisco, CA; Paul Dydman, USC Language Academy, CA; Anna Eddy, University of Michigan-Flint, MI; Zohan El-Gamal, Glendale Community College, CA; Jennie Farnell, University of Connecticut, CT; Susan Fedors, Howard Community College, MD; Valerie Fiechter, Mission College, CA; Ashley Fifer, Nassau County Community College, NY; Matthew Florence, Intrax International Institute, CA; Kathleen Flynn, Glendale College, CA; Elizabeth Fonsea, Nassau County Community College, NY; Eve Fonseca, St. Louis Community College, MO; Elizabeth Foss, Washtenaw Community College, MI; Duff C. Galda, Pima Community College, AZ; Christiane Galvani, Houston Community College, TX; Gretchen Gerber, Howard Community College, MD; Ray Gonzalez, Montgomery College, MD; Janet Goodwin, University of California, Los Angeles, CA; Alyona Gorokhova, Grossmont College, CA; John Graney, Santa Fe College, FL; Kathleen Green, Central High School, AZ; Nancy Hamadou, Pima Community College-West Campus, AZ; Webb Hamilton, De Anza College, San Jose City College, CA; Janet Harclerode, Santa Monica Community College, CA; Sandra Hartmann, Language and Culture Center, TX; Kathy Haven, Mission College, CA; Roberta Hendrick, Cuyahoga Community College, OH; Ginny Heringer, Pasadena City College, CA; Adam Henricksen, University of Maryland, MD; Carolyn Ho, Lone Star College-CyFair, TX; Peter Hoffman, LaGuardia Community College, NY; Linda Holden, College of Lake County, IL; Jana Holt, Lake Washington Technical College, WA; Antonio Iccarino, Boston University, MA; Gail Ibele, University of Wisconsin, WI; Nina Ito, American Language Institute, CSU Long Beach, CA; Linda Jensen, UCLA, CA; Lisa Jurkowitz, Pima Community College, CA; Mandy Kama, Georgetown University, Washington, DC; Stephanie Kasuboski, Cuyahoga Community College, OH; Chigusa Katoku, Mission College, CA; Sandra Kawamura, Sacramento City College, CA; Gail Kellersberger, University of Houston-Downtown, TX; Jane Kelly, Durham Technical Community College, NC; Maryanne Kildare, Nassau County Community College, NY; Julie Park Kim, George Mason University, VA; Kindra Kinyon, Los Angeles Trade-Technical College, CA; Matt Kline, El Camino College, CA; Lisa Kovacs-Morgan, University of California, San Diego, CA; Claudia Kupiec, DePaul University, IL; Renee La Rue, Lone Star College-Montgomery, TX; Janet Langon, Glendale College, CA; Lawrence Lawson, Palomar College, CA; Rachele Lawton, The Community College of Baltimore County, MD; Alice Lee, Richland College, TX; Esther S. Lee, CSUF & Mt. SAC, CA; Cherie Lenz-Hackett, University of Washington, WA; Joy Leventhal, Cuyahoga Community College, OH; Alice Lin, UCI Extension, CA; Monica Lopez, Cerritos College, CA; Dustin Lovell, FLS International Marymount College, CA; Carol Lowther, Palomar College, CA; Candace Lynch-Thompson, North Orange County Community College District, CA; Thi Thi Ma, City College of San Francisco, CA; Steve Mac Isaac, USC Long Academy, CA; Denise Maduli-Williams, City College of San Francisco, CA; Eileen Mahoney, Camelback High School, AZ; Naomi Mardock, MCC-Omaha, NE; Brigitte Maronde, Harold Washington College, IL; Marilyn Marquis, Laposita College CA; Doris Martin, Glendale Community College; Pasadena City College, CA; Keith Maurice, University of Texas at Arlington, TX; Nancy Mayer, University of Missouri-St. Louis, MO; Aziah McNamara, Kansas State University, KS; Billie McQuillan, Education Heights, MN; Karen Merritt, Glendale Union High School District, AZ; Holly Milkowart, Johnson County Community College, KS; Eric Moyer, Intrax International Institute, CA; Gino Muzzatti, Santa Rosa Junior College, CA; Sandra Navarro, Glendale Community College, CA; Melissa Nichelson, Pasadena City College, CA; Than Nyeinkhin, ELAC, PCC, CA; William Nedrow, Triton College, IL; Eric Nelson, University of Minnesota, MN; Than Nyeinkhin, ELAC, PCC, CA; Fernanda Ortiz, Center for English as a Second Language at the University of Arizona, AZ; Rhony Ory, Ygnacio Valley High School, CA; Paul Parent, Montgomery College, MD; Dr. Sumeeta Patnaik, Marshall University, WV; Oscar Pedroso, Miami Dade College, FL; Robin Persiani, Sierra College, CA; Patricia Prenz-Belkin, Hostos Community College, NY; Suzanne Powell, University of Louisville, KY;

iv

Hiroshima Kokusai Gakuin University, Japan; **Kevin Mueller**, Tokyo Kokusai Daigaku, Japan; **Hudson Murrell**, Baiko Gakuin University, Japan; **Frances Namba**, Senri International School of Kwansei Gakuin, Japan; **Keiichi Narita**, Niigata University, Japan; **Kim Chung Nguyen**, Ho Chi Minh University of Industry, Vietnam; **Do Thi Thanh Nhan**, Hanoi University, Vietnam; **Dale Kazuo Nishi**, Aoyama English Conversation School, Japan; **Huynh Thi Ai Nguyen**, Vietnam; **Dongshin Oh**, YBM PLS, South Korea; **Keiko Okada**, Dokkyo Daigaku, Japan; **Louise Ohashi**, Shukutoku University, Japan; **Yongjun Park**, Sangji University, South Korea; **Donald Patnaude**, Ajarn Donald's English Language Services, Thailand; **Virginia Peng**, Ritsumeikan University, Japan; **Suangkanok Piboonthamnont**, Rajamangala University of Technology, Thailand; **Simon Pitcher**, Business English Teaching Services, Japan; **John C. Probert**, New Education Worldwide, Thailand; **Do Thi Hoa Quyen**, Ton Duc Thang University, Vietnam; **John P. Racine**, Dokkyo University, Japan; **Kevin Ramsden**, Kyoto University of Foreign Studies, Japan; **Luis Rappaport**, Cung Thieu Nha Ha Noi, Vietnam; **Lisa Reshad**, Konan Daigaku Hyogo, Japan; **Peter Riley**, Taisho University, Japan; **Thomas N. Robb**, Kyoto Sangyo University, Japan; **Rory Rosszell**, Meiji Daigaku, Japan; **Maria Feti Rosyani**, Universitas Kristen Indonesia, Indonesia; **Greg Rouault**, Konan University, Japan; **Chris Ruddenklau**, Kindai University, Japan; **Hans-Gustav Schwartz**, Thailand; **Mary-Jane Scott**, Soongsil University, South Korea; **Dara Sheahan**, Seoul National University, South Korea; **James Sherlock**, A.P.W. Angthong, Thailand; **Prof. Shieh**, Minghsin University of Science & Technology, Xinfeng; **Yuko Shimizu**, Ritsumeikan University, Japan; **Suzila Mohd Shukor**, Universiti Sains Malaysia, Malaysia; **Stephen E. Smith**, Mahidol University, Thailand; **Moon-young Son**, South Korea; **Seunghee Son**, Anyang University, South Korea; **Mi-young Song**, Kyungwon University, South Korea; **Lisa Sood**, VUS, BIS, Vietnam; **Jason Stewart**, Taejon International Language School, South Korea; **Brian A. Stokes**, Korea University, South Korea; **Mulder Su**, Shih-Chien University, Kaohsiung; **Yoomi Suh**, English Plus, South Korea; **Yun-Fang Sun**, Wenzao Ursuline College of Languages, Kaohsiung; **Richard Swingle**, Kansai Gaidai University, Japan; **Sanford Taborn**, Kinjo Gakuin Daigaku, Japan; **Mamoru Takahashi**, Akita Prefectural University, Japan; **Tran Hoang Tan**, School of International Training, Vietnam; **Takako Tanaka**, Doshisha University, Japan; **Jeffrey Taschner**, American University Alumni Language Center, Thailand; **Matthew Taylor**, Kinjo Gakuin Daigaku, Japan; **Michael Taylor**, International Pioneers School, Thailand; **Kampanart Thammaphati**, Wattana Wittaya Academy, Thailand; **Tran Duong The**, Sao Mai Language Center, Vietnam; **Tran Dinh Tho**, Duc Tri Secondary School, Vietnam; **Huynh Thi Anh Thu**, Nhatrang College of Culture Arts and Tourism, Vietnam; **Peter Timmins**, Peter's English School, Japan; **Fumie Togano**, Hosei Daini High School, Japan; **F. Sigmund Topor**, Keio University Language School, Japan; **Tu Trieu**, Rise VN, Vietnam; **Yen-Cheng Tseng**, Chang-Jung Christian University, Tainan; **Pei-Hsuan Tu**, National Cheng Kung University, Tainan City; **Hajime Uematsu**, Hirosaki University, Japan; **Rachel Um**, Mok-dong Oedae English School, South Korea; **David Underhill**, EEExpress, Japan; **Ben Underwood**, Kugenuma High School, Japan; **Siriluck Usaha**, Sripatum University, Thailand; **Tyas Budi Utami**, Indonesia; **Nguyen Thi Van**, Far East International School, Vietnam; **Stephan Van Eycken**, Kosei Gakuen Girls High School, Japan; **Zisa Velasquez**, Taihu International School/Semarang International School, China/Indonesia; **Jeffery Walter**, Sangji University, South Korea; **Bill White**, Kinki University, Japan; **Yohanes De Deo Widyastoko**, Xaverius Senior High School, Indonesia; **Dylan Williams**, SNU, South Korea; **Jisuk Woo**, Ichean University, South Korea; **Greg Chung-Hsien Wu**, Providence University, Taichung; **Xun Xiaoming**, BLCU, China; **Hui-Lien Yeh**, Chai Nan University of Pharmacy and Science, Tainan; **Sittiporn Yodnil**, Huachiew Chalermprakiet University, Thailand; **Shamshul Helmy Zambahari**, Universiti Teknologi Malaysia, Malaysia; **Ming-Yuli**, Chang Jung Christian University, Tainan; **Aimin Fadhlee bin Mahmud Zuhodi**, Kuala Terengganu Science School, Malaysia;

TURKEY **Shirley F. Akis**, American Culture Association/Fomara; **Gül Akkoç**, Boğaziçi University; **Seval Akmeşe**, Haliç University; **Ayşenur Akyol**, Ege University; **Ayşe Umut Aribaş**, Beykent University; **Gökhan Asan**, Kapadokya Vocational College; **Hakan Asan**, Kapadokya Vocational College; **Julia Asan**, Kapadokya Vocational College; **Azarvan Atac**, Piri Reis University; **Nur Babat**, Kapadokya Vocational College; **Feyza Balakbabalar**, Kadir Has University; **Gözde Balikçi**, Beykent University; **Deniz Balım**, Haliç University; **Asli Başdoğan**, Kadir Has University; **Ayla Bayram**, Kapadokya Vocational College; **Pinar Bilgiç**, Kadir Has University; **Kenan Bozkurt**, Kapadokya Vocational College; **Yonca Bozkurt**, Ege University; **Frank Carr**, Piri Reis; **Mengü Noyan Çengel**, Ege University; **Elif Doğan**, Ege University; **Natalia Donmez**, 29 Mayis Üniversite; **Nalan Emirsoy**, Kadir Has University;

Ayşe Engin, Kadir Has University; **Ayhan Gedikbaş**, Ege University; **Gülşah Gençer**, Beykent University; **Seyit Ömer Gök**, Gediz University; **Tuğba Gök**, Gediz University; **İlkay Gökçe**, Ege University; **Zeynep Birinci Guler**, Maltepe University; **Neslihan Güler**, Kadir Has University; **Sircan Gümüş**, Kadir Has University; **Nesrin Gündoğu**, T.C. Piri Reis University; **Tanju Gurpinar**, Piri Reis University; **Selin Gurturk**, Piri Reis University; **Neslihan Gurutku**, Piri Reis University; **Roger Hewitt**, Maltepe University; **Nilüfer İbrahimoğlu**, Beykent University; **Nevin Kaftelen**, Kadir Has University; **Murat Kahraman**, Maltepe University; **Sultan Kalin**, Kapadokya Vocational College; **Sema Kaplan Karabina**, Anadolu University; **Eray Kara**, Giresun University; **Beylü Karayazgan**, Ege University; **Darren Kelso**, Piri Reis University; **Trudy Kittle**, Kapadokya Vocational College; **Şaziye Konaç**, Kadir Has University; **Güneş Korkmaz**, Kapadokya Vocational College; **Robert Ledbury**, Izmir University of Economics; **Ashley Lucas**, Maltepe University; **Bülent Nedium Uça**, Dogus University; **Murat Nurlu**, Ege University; **Mollie Owens**, Kadir Has University; **Oya Özağaç**, Boğaziçi University; **Funda Özcan**, Ege University; **İlkay Özdemir**, Ege University; **Ülkü Öztürk**, Gediz University; **Cassondra Puls**, Anadolu University; **Yelda Sarikaya**, Cappadocia Vocational College; **Müge Şekercioğlu**, Ege University; **Melis Senol**, Canakkale Onsekiz Mart University, The School of Foreign Languages; **Patricia Sümer**, Kadir Has University; **Rex Surface**, Beykent University; **Mustafa Torun**, Kapadokya Vocational College; **Tansel Üstünloğlu**, Ege University; **Fatih Yücel**, Beykent University; **Şule Yüksel**, Ege University;

THE MIDDLE EAST **Amina Saif Mohammed Al Hashamia**, Nizwa College of Applied Sciences, Oman; **Jennifer Baran**, Kuwait University, Kuwait; **Phillip Chappells**, GEMS Modern Academy, U.A.E.; **Sharon Ruth Devaneson**, Ibri College of Technology, Oman; **Hanaa El-Deeb**, Canadian International College, Egypt; **Yvonne Eaton**, Community College of Qatar, Qatar; **Brian Gay**, Sultan Qaboos University, Oman; **Gail Al Hafidh**, Sharjah Women's College (HCT), U.A.E.; **Jonathan Hastings**, American Language Center, Jordan; **Laurie Susan Hilu**, English Language Centre, University of Bahrain, Bahrain; **Abraham Irannezhad**, Mehre Aval, Iran; **Kevin Kempe**, CNA-Q, Qatar; **Jill Newby James**, University of Nizwa; **Mary Kay Klein**, American University of Sharjah, U.A.E.; **Sian Khoury**, Fujairah Women's College (HCT), U.A.E.; **Hussein Dehghan Manshadi**, Farhang Pajooh & Jaam-e-Jam Language School, Iran; **Jessica March**, American University of Sharjah, U.A.E.; **Neil McBeath**, Sultan Qaboos University, Oman; **Sandy McDonagh**, Abu Dhabi Men's College (HCT), U.A.E.; **Rob Miles**, Sharjah Women's College (HCT), U.A.E.; **Michael Kevin Neumann**, Al Ain Men's College (HCT), U.A.E.;

LATIN AMERICA **Aldana Aguirre**, Argentina; **Claudia Almeida**, Coordenação de Idiomas, Brazil; **Cláudia Arias**, Brazil; **Maria de los Angeles Barba**, FES Acatlan UNAM, Mexico; **Lilia Barrios**, Universidad Autónoma de Tamaulipas, Mexico; **Adán Beristain**, UAEM, Mexico; **Ricardo Böck**, Manoel Ribas, Brazil; **Edson Braga**, CNA, Brazil; **Marli Buttelli**, Mater et Magistra, Brazil; **Alessandra Campos**, Inova Centro de Linguas, Brazil; **Priscila Catta Preta Ribeiro**, Brazil; **Gustavo Cestari**, Access International School, Brazil; **Walter D'Alessandro**, Virginia Language Center, Brazil; **Lilian De Gennaro**, Argentina; **Mônica De Stefani**, Quality Centro de Idiomas, Brazil; **Julio Alejandro Flores**, BUAP, Mexico; **Mirian Freire**, CNA Vila Guilherme, Brazil; **Francisco Garcia**, Colegio Lestonnac de San Angel, Mexico; **Miriam Giovanardi**, Brazil; **Darlene Gonzalez Miy**, ITESM CCV, Mexico; **Maria Laura Grimaldi**, Argentina; **Luz Dary Guzmán**, IMPAHU, Colombia; **Carmen Koppe**, Brazil; **Monica Krutzler**, Brazil; **Marcus Murilo Lacerda**, Seven Idiomas, Brazil; **Nancy Lake**, CEL-LEP, Brazil; **Cris Lazzerini**, Brazil; **Sandra Luna**, Argentina; **Ricardo Luvisan**, Brazil; **Jorge Murilo Menezes**, ACBEU, Brazil; **Monica Navarro**, Instituto Cultural A. C., Mexico; **Joacyr Oliveira**, Faculdades Metropolitanas Unidas and Summit School for Teachers, Brazil; **Ayrton Cesar Oliveira de Araujo**, E&A English Classes, Brazil; **Ana Laura Oriente**, Seven Idiomas, Brazil; **Adelia Peña Clavel**, CELE UNAM, Mexico; **Beatriz Pereira**, Summit School, Brazil; **Miguel Perez**, Instituto Cultural, Mexico; **Cristiane Perone**, Associação Cultura Inglesa, Brazil; **Pamela Claudia Pogré**, Colegio Integral Caballito / Universidad de Flores, Argentina; **Dalva Prates**, Brazil; **Marianne Rampaso**, Iowa Idiomas, Brazil; **Daniela Rutolo**, Instituto Superior Cultural Británico, Argentina; **Maione Sampaio**, Maione Carrijo Consultoria em Inglês Ltda, Brazil; **Elaine Santesso**, TS Escola de Idiomas, Brazil; **Camila Francisco Santos**, UNS Idiomas, Brazil; **Lucia Silva**, Cooplem Idiomas, Brazil; **Maria Adela Sorzio**, Instituto Superior Santa Cecilia, Argentina; **Elcio Souza**, Unibero, Brazil; **Willie Thomas**, Rainbow Idiomas, Brazil; **Sandra Villegas**, Instituto Humberto de Paolis, Argentina; **John Whelan**, La Universidad Nacional Autonoma de Mexico, Mexico

CONTENTS

UNIT 1

Sociology

NOTE TAKING	▶	using notes to summarize a lecture
LISTENING	▶	making inferences
VOCABULARY	▶	suffixes
GRAMMAR	▶	auxiliary verbs *do, be, have*
PRONUNCIATION	▶	contractions with auxiliary verbs
SPEAKING	▶	taking conversational turns

UNIT QUESTION

Are first impressions accurate?

A Discuss these questions with your classmates.

1. What do you notice when you meet someone for the first time?

2. How important do you think first impressions are? Why?

3. Look at the photo. What do you think of this person from just looking at him? Do you think your first impression is accurate? Why or why not?

B Listen to *The Q Classroom* online. Then answer these questions.

1. How did the students answer the question? Do you agree or disagree with their ideas? Why?

2. What are some other ways that a person can give a good impression? What are some ways that a person can give a bad impression?

iQ ONLINE   **C** Go to the Online Discussion Board to discuss the Unit Question with your classmates.

UNIT
OBJECTIVE ▶▶▶▶ Listen to a lecture and an excerpt from a radio show
and gather information and ideas to describe in detail
an accurate first impression.

D Read the proverbs (sayings). Decide whether each proverb means that first impressions are *accurate* (A) or *not accurate* (N). Discuss your answers with a partner. Look up any unfamiliar words in the dictionary.

_____ 1. Don't judge a horse by its saddle. (Arabic)

_____ 2. Faces we see; hearts we don't know. (Spanish)

_____ 3. What you see is what you get. (English)

_____ 4. You must judge a man by the work of his hands. (African)

_____ 5. Never judge a book by its cover. (English)

_____ 6. A tree starts with a seed. (Arabic)

_____ 7. If it walks like a duck and quacks like a duck, it's a duck. (English)

_____ 8. Don't think there are no crocodiles because the water is calm. (Malaysian)

E Do you have any proverbs in your culture about first impressions? What are they? Tell your partner.

F Which proverbs from Activity D do you think are the truest? Discuss your ideas with your partner.

A good way to remember a lecture is to put the key ideas into your own words. This will also help you confirm that you understood all the information and that your notes are complete.

As soon as possible after a lecture, put the key, or most important, ideas into your own words, and say them out loud to a study partner or to yourself. Saying them out loud will help you clarify the ideas and remember them better.

Imagine this situation: Your friend had to miss class because he was ill. The next day, he asks you to tell him about the lecture. What would you tell him?

You would probably give him the following information: مها ضرہ

- the topic of the lecture
- the main ideas
- a few important points and examples

This is the same information that you use when you summarize. A **summary** is a shorter version of the information that includes all of the main ideas, but only a few details.

Here are some phrases that are used as signposts.

- *The professor talked about . . .*
- *She explained . . .*
- *She told us . . .*
- *Then he discussed . . .*
- *He gave us the example of . . .*
- *After that he wrapped up with . . .*

A. Read this excerpt from a lecture on first impressions. Then answer the questions.

When you meet someone for the first time, you want to be remembered in a positive way. One way to make a good first impression is to listen. Sometimes speakers talk too much and don't listen. Show interest and ask questions. What does the other person like to do? Where is he or she from? What is his or her family like?

Second, use body language effectively. What does this mean? Show you are paying attention by leaning in, maintaining eye contact, and using facial expressions. Smile, raise your eyebrows, and tilt your head. Through your use of questions and body language, you can make a good first impression.

1. What is the topic? _How to make *a good* a first impression._

2. What two main points does the speaker make?

   ~~~~ Listen

   Show intrest and asks question.

3. What is one detail that illustrates each main point?

   _____

   _____

B. With a partner, take turns summarizing the lecture excerpt.

 **C.** Go online for more practice using notes to summarize a lecture.

home munke

LISTENING 1 | The Psychology of First Impressions

You are going to listen to a lecture about first impressions. As you listen to the lecture, gather information and ideas about first impressions.

PREVIEW THE LISTENING

Tip for Success

Presentations and talks often begin with a short story or anecdote. The story is usually an example of the topic the speaker is going to talk about.

A. **PREVIEW** A psychologist will explain how first impressions affect our opinion of a new person. Check (✓) the statement about first impressions you think is true.

☐ First impressions give us a good idea of what a person is really like.

☐ We often make errors because of first impressions.

B. **VOCABULARY** Read aloud these words from Listening 1. Check (✓) the ones you know. Use a dictionary to define any new or unknown words. Then discuss with a partner how the words will relate to the unit.

assume (v.) 🔑	form an impression (phr.)
behavior (n.) 🔑	negative (adj.) 🔑
briefly (adv.) 🔑	positive (adj.) 🔑
encounter (n.) 🔑	sample (n.) 🔑
error (n.) 🔑	trait (n.)

🔑 Oxford 3000™ words

C. Go online to listen and practice your pronunciation.

WORK WITH THE LISTENING

A. **LISTEN AND TAKE NOTES** Listen to the lecture about first impressions. Before you listen, look at the outline below. As you listen, add the topic and important details.

Topic: _How to make first Impressions_

Example: Waiting in line at a coffee shop

Main idea: Impressions of others

Detail(s)

First mistake: _____

Second mistake: _____

Main idea: When we view our own behavior

Detail: It's not our personality; it's the _____.

B. Work with a partner. Take turns using your notes to summarize the lecture.

C. Read the statements. Write *T* (true) or *F* (false). Then correct each false statement to make it true.

1. _F_ First impressions tell the whole story.

   First impressions tell only part of the story. _____

2. _F_ If a person is happy when we meet her, we will often think she is happy all the time.

   _____

3. ____ Our first impressions give us an accurate picture of the whole person.

   _____

4. _T_ We judge other people's behavior differently from our own.

   _____

🔊 **D. Read the sentences. Then listen again. Circle the answer or answers that best complete each statement.**

1. People _____ what they see in a first encounter.
   (a.) often make mistakes about
   b. make sense of information from
   c. form very accurate impressions from

2. People assume that their first impressions tell them about _____ person.
   a. a sample of a
   b. most of a
   (c.) the whole

3. If we think a person is happy when we first meet her, we will think she is also _____.
   (a.) friendly
   b. boring
   c. kind

4. If someone else does something negative, we think _____ .

    a. it is because of his personality

    b. he is a bad person

    c. it is because of how he felt that day

5. If we do something negative, we think it is because of _____ .

    a. our personality

    b. the situation

    c. someone else

E. Check (✓) the statements you think the lecturer agrees with. Discuss your answers with a partner. Support your arguments with information from the lecture.

    ☐ 1. If a stranger behaves rudely, you may assume he isn't intelligent.

    ☐ 2. First impressions are rarely accurate.

    ☐ 3. People make more excuses for their own bad behavior.

    ☐ 4. An example of behavior can tell us a lot about someone's personality.

F. Read the text below. Discuss the questions with a partner.

On my first day of college, I was moving into my dorm room when my roommate, Renee, came in. She had already moved in and taken the bed by the window. Her stuff was everywhere. Her parents were with her. They were very nice and introduced themselves, but Renee was quiet and didn't really look at me. I didn't say much either because I thought she didn't like me. She threw her bag on her bed and they all left. I was very upset. I thought Renee was rude and mean. I was mad that she didn't even give me a chance.

An hour or so later, Renee came back to the room. She apologized for her rudeness. She had just had a bad argument with her parents and was upset with them. She described their fight in a very funny way, and we both laughed. After that, she became one of my best friends. She's the perfect roommate.

    1. How accurate was the writer's first impression of her roommate?

        It was not accurate at all

    2. How does this story illustrate the points the speaker made in her lecture?

G. Go online to listen to *First Impressions from Photos* and check your comprehension.

Tip for Success

Pay attention to articles. They come before nouns and help you identify parts of speech.

H. **VOCABULARY** Use the new vocabulary from Listening 1. Complete each sentence with the correct word or phrase.

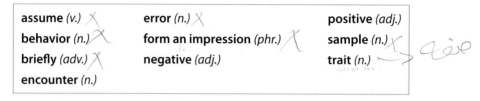

assume (v.) ✗   error (n.) ✗   positive (adj.)

behavior (n.) ✗   form an impression (phr.) ✗   sample (n.) ✗

briefly (adv.) ✗   negative (adj.)   trait (n.)

encounter (n.)

1. I took a(n) _____sample_____ of the carpet home to see whether I liked the color in my living room.

2. Alberto made several _____errors_____ on his math test because he didn't study hard enough.

3. Luisa said she wasn't feeling well, so I _____assume_____ she's not going out tonight.

4. The teacher went over yesterday's assignment very _____briefly_____. We only spent about fifteen minutes on it, so I still have some questions.

5. When I meet new people, I watch their _____behavior_____ closely to see what they are like.

6. It only takes a few minutes to _____form an impression_____ of someone you meet for the first time.

7. One _____negative_____ thing about moving to a new place is leaving your friends and family behind.

8. Most of my good friends have one personality _____trait_____ in common—they are all very funny.

9. Do you usually have a(n) _____positive_____ feeling about people when you meet them for the first time? I do because I think most people are good.

10. My first _____encounter_____ with my new neighbors was very unpleasant. We argued about the amount of noise they were making.

I. Go online for more practice with the vocabulary.

SAY WHAT YOU THINK

Discuss the questions in a group.

1. In this lecture, the speaker says we often think that the way a person behaves when we first meet him is the way he behaves all the time. From your personal experience, do you agree or disagree? Give examples.

2. Have you ever formed a first impression of someone that was wrong? Explain.

Making inferences means to draw conclusions about information that is not stated directly by using information that you already know or that is stated directly. Making inferences while listening can help deepen your understanding of what you hear.

Listen to a student talking about meeting his professor for the first time.

> When I first met my professor, he shook my hand firmly and then asked me questions about myself. He was very polite. He also was relaxed and seemed interested in what I was saying.

Even though the student does not state directly that his first impression of his professor was positive, you can infer or conclude that he did from the information he does state directly.

- He shook my hand firmly.
- He asked questions.
- He was relaxed and seemed interested.

A. Listen to a student talk about a first impression. Take notes in your notebook as you listen. Then answer the questions.

Form shock

1. Do you think it was a positive or negative first impression? Why? What information from your notes helped you answer?

   He's late wise sit wit us

   POSITIVE

2. Do you think the speaker likes Lee? Why? What information from your notes helped you answer?

   yes / # he waive t hhim.

B. Work with a partner. Compare your answers.

C. Listen to the speaker's opinion of Lee. Take notes in your notebook. Compare what the speaker says about Lee with your answers in Activity A.

D. Work with a partner. Tell a story about meeting someone for the first time. Describe what she or he did and a few things you noticed. Don't say how you felt about the person. Ask your partner to infer whether your impression was positive or negative.

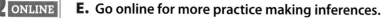

E. Go online for more practice making inferences.

LISTENING 2 | Book Review of *Blink* by Malcolm Gladwell

You are going to listen to an excerpt from a radio show in which a critic reviews a book. The book discusses the types of decisions we make as a result of first impressions. As you listen to the excerpt, gather information and ideas about first impressions.

PREVIEW THE LISTENING

A. PREVIEW Check (✓) which things, if any, you could easily make a quick decision about.

☐ a book to read   ☐ a new pair of shoes

☐ a DVD to watch   ☐ a place to go on vacation

☐ a new car   ☐ a restaurant

B. VOCABULARY Read aloud these words from Listening 2. Check (✓) the ones you know. Use a dictionary to define any new or unknown words. Then discuss with a partner how the words will relate to the unit.

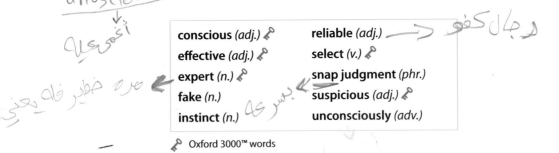

unoscious

conscious *(adj.)* 🔑   **reliable** *(adj.)*

effective *(adj.)* 🔑   **select** *(v.)* 🔑

expert *(n.)* 🔑   **snap judgment** *(phr.)*

fake *(n.)*   **suspicious** *(adj.)* 🔑

instinct *(n.)*   **unconsciously** *(adv.)*

🔑 Oxford 3000™ words

iQ ONLINE **C.** Go online to listen and practice your pronunciation.

WORK WITH THE LISTENING

🔊 **A.** LISTEN AND TAKE NOTES Listen to the book review of *Blink* by Malcolm Gladwell. Before you listen, look at the partial outline below. As you listen, take notes on the main ideas, examples, and other details. After the listening is over, go back and add to or edit your notes for clarity.

Topic: Malcolm Gladwell's *Blink*

Main idea: Gladwell thinks first impressions are usually __reliable__.

Example:

Two ways we make decisions

1. __slowly and civeLy__ with our conscious minds

2. quickly, or __un conscious__

Research on accurate first impressions

Students watched videos of _____*a teacher*_____, could tell

how _____*effective*_____ they would be.

People could look at _____*room*_____ and learn

about _____*character*_____.

Examples of decision-making

Careful: _____

Snap: _____

B. With a partner, take turns summarizing the review from your notes.

C. Complete the chart. Use your notes from activity A. Compare charts with a partner.

Main ideas	Examples or details
First impressions are _____*reliable*_____.	
Unconscious decisions are _____*quickly*_____.	
Conscious decisions are _____*slow and circle*_____.	

D. Listen again. Match each detail with an example given in the review. Then put the details in the order you heard them.

Examples
a. selecting a soccer player
b. looking at a bedroom
c. buying something for the kitchen
d. watching a video
e. writing down the first word that comes to mind

Details   Order you heard in the report

____ an easy decision   *4*

____ describing someone's character   *3*

____ recognizing a fake artifact   *1*

____ judging a teacher's effectiveness   *2*

____ a difficult decision with a lot of information *5*

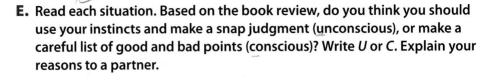

depend

E. Read each situation. Based on the book review, do you think you should use your instincts and make a snap judgment (unconscious), or make a careful list of good and bad points (conscious)? Write *U* or *C*. Explain your reasons to a partner.

1. buying a coffee maker _U_

2. choosing a study partner _U_

3. asking someone on the street for help _C_

4. choosing vegetable seeds for your garden _C_

5. buying a car _C_

6. choosing a seat on a train _C_

F. Read more information below on first impressions from two researchers. With a partner, discuss five tips you can give others on making first impressions. Use this information and the information from *Blink*.

Nalini Ambady was a researcher at Tufts University. She did a study on how well students could make judgments about instructors from a short video. According to Ambady, when people think more before making a decision, the decisions tend not to be as good as when they make them unconsciously.

Frank Bernieri of Oregon State University says that research suggests that people who are more confident about their judgments of people are actually less accurate. He advises people to try to convince themselves of the opposite point of view. For example, if you assume someone is rude and unkind, you should try to see his or her behavior in a completely different way.

Tips:

_____

_____

_____

_____

_____

G. **VOCABULARY** Use the new vocabulary from Listening 2. Read the sentences. Circle the answer that best matches the meaning of each bold word or phrase.

1. I make a **conscious** effort to stay in regular contact with all my friends. I make time to call and email them often.
   a. accidental   b. intentional   c. occasional

2. Watching a video is an **effective** way to study someone's behavior. You can learn a lot from the way people move their hands.
   a. successful   b. interesting   c. unusual

3. Marcos is an **expert** at swimming. He has been doing it a long time.
   a. beginner   b. failure   c. skillful person

4. The artifact was a **fake**. It was not thousands of years old.
   a. an imitation   b. a problem   c. an original

5. When you meet new people, you should trust your **instincts**. Your first reaction is often correct.
   a. natural feelings   b. general knowledge   c. careful research

6. My car isn't **reliable**. There is always something wrong with it.
   a. dependable   b. expensive   c. comfortable

7. I can't **select** anyone to receive the award. There are too many good students.
   a. tell   b. call   c. choose

8. I often make **snap judgments** about things I buy. I don't like to waste time.
   a. careful decisions   b. bad decisions   c. quick decisions

9. My parents were **suspicious** when I told them the teacher did not give any grades for our assignment.
   a. uninterested   b. doubtful   c. excited

10. I was so focused on listening to the news this morning that I **unconsciously** poured orange juice in my coffee instead of milk.
    a. without thinking   b. without caring   c. without studying

H. Go online for more practice with the vocabulary.

SAY WHAT YOU THINK

A. Discuss the questions in a group.

1. Malcolm Gladwell suggests that we should make difficult decisions more quickly and with our unconscious minds. Do you agree with him? Why or why not?

2. According to Gladwell, our first impressions are often reliable. Do you think this is true? Why or why not?

B. Before you watch the video, discuss the questions in a group.

1. In which situations are first impressions really important?

2. How do you want to present yourself in a job interview?

iQ ONLINE

C. Go online to watch a video about the mistakes people make in a job interview. Then check your comprehension.

Critical Thinking Tip

Activity D asks you to **compare** and **contrast** job interviews with other types of first impressions. You compare ideas that are the same. You contrast ideas that are different. **Comparing** and **contrasting** can help you understand the ways in which job interviews are similar to or different from other types of first impressions.

D. Think about the unit video, Listening 1, and Listening 2 as you discuss the questions.

1. In what kinds of situations do you think first impressions are usually accurate?

2. In what ways are job interviews similar to other types of first impressions people make? How are they different?

We form first impressions wherever we are.

Use **suffixes** and other word endings to help you recognize parts of speech. Recognizing the part of speech will help you guess the meaning of an unfamiliar word. It will also help you expand your vocabulary as you notice other parts of speech in the same word family.

Common noun suffixes: *-acy, -er/-or, -ment, -ness, -tion*

accur**acy**, research**er**, invent**or**, amuse**ment**, friendli**ness**, atten**tion**

Common verb suffixes: *-ate, -en, -ize*

stimul**ate**, strength**en**, energ**ize**

Common adjective suffixes: *-able, -al, -ful, -ive, -ous*

depend**able**, tradition**al**, care**ful**, effect**ive**, humor**ous**

Common adverb suffixes: *-ly, -ally*

particular**ly**, univers**ally**

A. Look at the new words. For each word, write the suffix, the part of speech, and the base word from which the new word is formed.

New word	Suffix	Part of speech	Base word
1. accuracy	-acy	noun	accurate
2. assumption	-tion	noun	assum
3. consciously	-ly	adverb	conscious
4. prediction	-tion	noun	product
5. effectively	ly	adverb	effective
6. instinctive	ive	adjective	instinct
7. selection	tion	noun	select

B. Work with a partner. Discuss the meanings of the new words from Activity A. Then use a dictionary to check the definitions of any words you are not sure of.

C. Complete each sentence with the correct word from Activity A.

1. That bookstore offers a great ___selection___ of classic literature. There are so many, it's hard to choose!

2. ___accuracy___ is really important in grammar, so you should try not to make mistakes.

3. We often make ___assumption___ about people because of the way they look. Then we sometimes discover that our first impressions were incorrect.

4. I don't pay much attention to weather reports. Their ___prediction___ are usually wrong. It was supposed to be sunny yesterday, but it rained all day!

5. If an advertisement is ___effectively___ designed, sales of the product will increase.

6. Many animals have a(n) ___instinctive___ fear of fire and the danger it represents. They don't learn it. It's part of their nature.

7. I have to make decisions very _____ when I go shopping. If I don't, I buy things I really don't need without even realizing it.

iQ ONLINE **D.** Go online for more practice with suffixes.

SPEAKING

 **UNIT OBJECTIVE** ▶▶▶▶ At the end of this unit, you will give a short talk to a partner about a first impression. Make sure to take conversational turns when you talk to your partner.

Grammar — Auxiliary verbs *do, be, have*

The **auxiliary verbs** *do, be,* and *have* are used to make questions and negative statements.

Use *do* with the simple present and simple past.

Simple present
Does he like pizza?
He **doesn't** like pizza.

Simple past
Did they bring their books?
They **didn't** bring their books.

Use *be* with the present and past continuous.

Present continuous
Are you reading?
We **aren't** reading now.

Past continuous
Was Mr. Knight teaching here last year?
He **wasn't** teaching here last year.

Use *have* with the present perfect.

Present perfect
Has she left yet?
Nancy **hasn't** left yet.

A. Rewrite the sentences as negative statements. Use the correct form of *do, be,* or *have* as the auxiliary verb.

1. I often make snap judgments.

   I don't often make snap judgments.

2. Bill thinks first impressions about teachers are usually accurate.

   Bill doesn't

3. Sara trusted her instincts when meeting new people.

   Sara did idnt

4. When Waleed buys something, he usually thinks about it for a long time.

   _____ doesn't _____

5. Jenny is working hard this week.

_____ is not _____

6. I've formed a positive impression of that company.

_____ I haven't _____

B. Rewrite the sentences as questions. Use the correct form of *do, be,* or *have* as the auxiliary verb.

1. You have made many incorrect assumptions because of how someone looked.

   Have you made many incorrect assumptions because of how someone looked?

2. I like talking to new people on the phone.

   _____ Do you _____

3. Ross is living with people he met last year.

   _____ is Ross _____

4. Hatem made lots of friends at school.

   _____ did Hatem makes _____

5. The experts realized the artifact was a fake.

   _____

6. Jamal has selected his library books already.

   _____ has Jaml _____

C. Work with a partner. Take turns asking and answering the questions from Activity B. Use auxiliary verbs in your short answers.

A: Do you like talking to new people on the phone?
B: Yes, I do./No, I don't.

D. Go online for more practice with auxiliary verbs.

E. Go online for the grammar expansion.

Auxiliary verbs are usually unstressed and can be shortened as part of a **contraction**. Most contractions can be used in speech and informal writing, but some are only used in speech.

Listen to these examples of contractions.

Contractions used in speech or writing

> She's eating now. (She is eating now.)
> They're watching TV. (They are watching TV.)
> Lisa's already left. (Lisa has already left.)
> We've finished our work. (We have finished our work.)

Contractions used only in speech

> What's it cost? (What does it cost?)
> Where'd you go? (Where did you go?)
> Why'd he arrive so late? (Why did he arrive so late?)

A. Listen to these sentences with contractions. Write the full form of the auxiliary verb.

1. Who ___is___ your favorite author?

2. Where ___did___ you go on your last vacation?

3. Mary ___is___ going to the store.

4. Jack ___is___ gone already.

5. We ___have___ usually eaten by 6:00.

6. What ___did___ you do after class yesterday?

7. The girls ___have___ been here before.

B. Work with a partner. Take turns saying the sentences from Activity A. Use the full form of the auxiliary verbs. Then practice saying them with contractions.

iQ ONLINE **C.** Go online for more practice with contractions with auxiliary verbs.

When you are speaking with someone, it is polite to take turns talking. Taking turns keeps the conversation going and shows that you are interested in what the other person is saying.

If the other person asks you a question, answer it, and add some new information. If possible, ask a question of your own. Here are some questions you can use.

What do you think?	How about you?
Do you agree?	You know?
Right?	OK?

A. Complete the conversation with questions from the Speaking Skill box. Then practice the conversation with a partner.

Tony: Hi. I'm Tony. It's nice to meet you.

Alex: My name's Alex. Nice to meet you too. Are you a new student?

Tony: No. I've been studying here for two years.

_____ How abot you _____
1

Alex: I just started this week, but so far, this class looks interesting.

_____ Do you agree _____
2

Tony: I agree. The teacher's very effective. The book he's using looks good, too.

_____ what do you think _____
3

Alex: Yeah. He seems friendly and interesting.

B. Read the questions and write notes in your notebook to help you answer. Then have a conversation about each question with a partner. Keep the conversations going for at least three turns each, and signal your partner's turn by using questions from the Speaking Skill box.

1. Who was your most effective teacher when you were a child? What impressed you about him or her?

2. Have you ever made a bad first impression on someone else? What did you do?

iQ ONLINE **C.** Go online for more practice with taking conversational turns.

Living in stolte is not easy

I'm having a good time.

برديسسسس

UNIT OBJECTIVE ▶▶▶▶

In this assignment, you are going to give a talk to a partner about a first impression. As you prepare your talk, think about the Unit Question, "Are first impressions accurate?" Use information from Listening 1, Listening 2, the unit video, and your work in this unit to support your talk. Refer to the Self-Assessment checklist on page 24.

CONSIDER THE IDEAS

Which items in the chart tell you the most about new people when you are forming a first impression? Check (✓) whether you think each item is very important, important, or not important. Then compare and discuss your answers with a partner.

	Very important	Important	Not important
their level of politeness	☐	☐	☐
their clothing	☐	☐	☐
their hairstyle	☐	☐	☐
their voice	☐	☐	☐
their eye contact	☐	☐	☐
their attitude to money	☐	☐	☐
the way they drive	☐	☐	☐
their job	☐	☐	☐
their likes and dislikes	☐	☐	☐
Your own ideas:			
	☐	☐	☐
	☐	☐	☐

PREPARE AND SPEAK

A. **GATHER IDEAS**   Complete these steps.

1. Think about a time when your first impression of someone was incorrect.

2. Brainstorm as much as you can remember about the situation.

3. Then write what you thought about the person when you first met and how your first impression was wrong.

B. ORGANIZE IDEAS Use your ideas from Activity A to help you answer these questions. Do not write full sentences. Just write notes to help you remember your answers.

Who was the person? _____

Where, when, and why did you meet? _____

What was your first impression? _____

Why did you form this impression? _____

When did you realize your first impression was wrong? _____

What changed your mind? _____

What do you think about the person now? _____

C. SPEAK Tell your partner about your first impression of the person you chose. Refer to the Self-Assessment checklist before you begin.

1. Explain why you formed that impression and why you were wrong.

2. You can refer to your notes, but do not read exactly what you wrote.

3. Talk for at least one minute.

iQ ONLINE **Go online for your alternate Unit Assignment.**

CHECK AND REFLECT

A. CHECK Think about the Unit Assignment as you complete the Self-Assessment checklist.

Yes	No	SELF-ASSESSMENT
☐	☐	I was able to speak easily about the topic.
☐	☐	My partner understood me.
☐	☐	I used vocabulary from the unit.
☐	☐	I used auxiliary verbs and contractions.
☐	☐	I took turns when speaking.

B. REFLECT Go to the Online Discussion Board to discuss these questions.

1. What is something new you learned in this unit?

2. Look back at the Unit Question—Are first impressions accurate? Is your answer different now than when you started this unit? If yes, how is it different? Why?

TRACK YOUR SUCCESS

[handwritten: don't / act → تمثيل   لا تمثل   tornido → عاصفة قوية / storm →]

Circle the words and phrases you have learned in this unit.

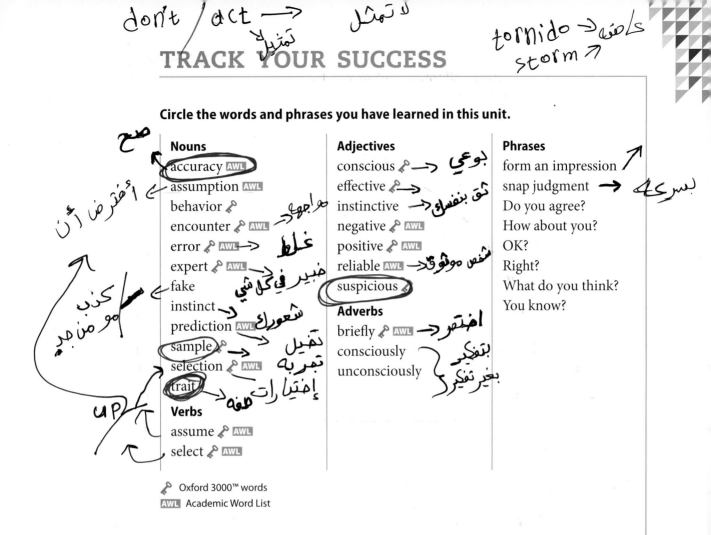

Nouns
accuracy AWL *[circled]*
assumption AWL
behavior 🔑
encounter 🔑 AWL
error 🔑 AWL
expert 🔑 AWL
fake
instinct
prediction AWL
sample 🔑 *[circled]*
selection 🔑 AWL
trait *[circled]*

Verbs
assume 🔑 AWL
select 🔑 AWL

Adjectives
conscious 🔑
effective 🔑
instinctive
negative 🔑 AWL
positive 🔑 AWL
reliable AWL
suspicious 🔑 *[circled]*

Adverbs
briefly 🔑 AWL
consciously
unconsciously

Phrases
form an impression
snap judgment
Do you agree?
How about you?
OK?
Right?
What do you think?
You know?

🔑 Oxford 3000™ words
AWL Academic Word List

Check (✓) the skills you learned. If you need more work on a skill, refer to the page(s) in parentheses.

NOTE TAKING	☐ I can use my notes to summarize a lecture. (p. 5)
LISTENING	☐ I can make inferences. (p. 11)
VOCABULARY	☐ I can use suffixes. (p. 17)
GRAMMAR	☐ I can use the auxiliary verbs *do, be,* and *have.* (p. 19)
PRONUNCIATION	☐ I can use contractions with auxiliary verbs. (p. 21)
SPEAKING	☐ I can take conversational turns. (p. 22)
UNIT OBJECTIVE ▶▶▶▶	☐ I can gather information and ideas to describe in detail an accurate first impression.

UNIT **2**

Nutritional Science

LISTENING ▶ listening for causes and effects
NOTE TAKING ▶ taking notes on causes and effects
VOCABULARY ▶ adjective-noun collocations
GRAMMAR ▶ quantifiers with count/noncount nouns
PRONUNCIATION ▶ links with /j/ and /w/
SPEAKING ▶ giving advice

Q

UNIT QUESTION

What's more important: taste or nutrition?

A Discuss these questions with your classmates.

1. How important is food in your life? Do you "eat to live" or "live to eat"?

2. Do you agree that if something tastes great, it's probably bad for you?

3. Look at the photo. What can you tell about these people's attitude about food and nutrition?

UNIT
OBJECTIVE ▶▶▶▶ Listen to an interview and a talk and gather
information and ideas to conduct a class survey
on food preferences.

◉ **B** Listen to *The Q Classroom* online. Then
match the ideas in the box to the students.

a. we need food that is both healthy and tastes good

b. eating healthy food is important

c. good nutrition makes people healthy

d. food that tastes good makes people happy

The importance of taste and nutrition	
Sophy	b. eating healthy food is important
Felix	
Marcus	
Yuna	

iQ ONLINE **C** Go to the Online Discussion Board to discuss the Unit Question with
your classmates.

D Read the paragraph and complete the chart.

A Matter of Taste

For a long time, experts in the West believed there were only four basic tastes: *sweet, sour, salty,* and *bitter*. Then, in the early 2000s, *umami* was recognized as the fifth basic taste. *Umami* is a Japanese word that means "yummy" or "nice." It describes food that tastes "meaty," such as meat, fish, and cheese.

bananas

ice cream

grapefruit

pickle

nuts

coffee

radish

lemon

Look at the pictures. Where do you think each food or drink should go? Complete the chart. Then check (✔) your favorite foods.

parsley

pineapple

chicken

potato chips

Sweet	Sour	Salty	Bitter	Umami
ice cream	grapefruit	potato chips	coffee	chicken

E Compare your answers in a group. Do you all agree which basic taste each food has? Add some more examples to the chart.

F Check (✓) your favorite foods in the chart. Which of the five basic tastes do you like best? Who in your group shares your sense of taste?

LISTENING 1 | You Are What You Eat

UNIT OBJECTIVE ▶▶▶▶

You are going to listen to an excerpt from a radio show in which Andrew Patterson interviews Dr. Maureen O'Ryan, a nutrition expert. As you listen to the excerpt, gather information and ideas about the importance of taste and nutrition.

PREVIEW THE LISTENING

Critical Thinking **Tip**

Activity A asks you to make predictions. When you make predictions, you use what you already know to help you guess the answers.

A. **PREVIEW** Look at this list of foods and drinks. Which do you think have good effects? Which have bad effects? Write *G* (good) or *B* (bad). Then compare your ideas with a classmate. Which of these foods and drinks do you consume most in your diet?

cheese ____

coffee ____

dark chocolate ____

milk chocolate ____

red meat ____

soda ____

tea ____

white meat ____

B. **VOCABULARY** Read aloud these words from Listening 1. Check (✓) the ones you know. Use a dictionary to find the meaning of any words you do not know. Then discuss with a partner how these words may relate to the unit.

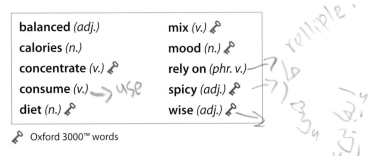

balanced *(adj.)*
calories *(n.)*
concentrate *(v.)* 🔑
consume *(v.)* → use
diet *(n.)* 🔑

mix *(v.)* 🔑
mood *(n.)* 🔑
rely on *(phr. v.)*
spicy *(adj.)* 🔑
wise *(adj.)* 🔑

🔑 Oxford 3000™ words

 ONLINE **C.** Go online to listen and practice your pronunciation.

WORK WITH THE LISTENING

A **LISTEN AND TAKE NOTES** Choose one of the foods or drinks from Activity A in Preview the Listening on page 29. Listen to the interview and take notes on what Dr. O'Ryan says about it. Then tell your partner.

Food or drink: _____

Notes: _____

_____

B. Listen again to the interview. What does Dr. O'Ryan say about each food or drink? Check (✓) the correct answer.

	Better for you	OK in small amounts	Bad for you
1. red meat			
2. white meat			
3. cheese			
4. coffee			
5. tea			
6. soda			
7. milk chocolate			
8. dark chocolate			

C. Read the sentences. Circle the answer that best completes each statement.

1. Dr. O'Ryan's advice is to _____.
   a. eat anything you like
   b. always eat healthy foods
   c. eat a balanced diet

2. Red meat is good for your _____.
   a. eyesight
   b. hair and teeth
   c. bones and skin

3. Eating turkey can help you _____.
   a. feel more relaxed
   b. lose more weight
   c. have better eyesight

4. Cheese can raise your blood pressure because it contains a lot of _____.
   a. oil
   b. salt
   c. calories

5. Too much coffee can _____.
   a. make you feel stressed
   b. give you too much energy
   c. affect your heart

6. Green tea can help you _____.
   a. lose weight
   b. sleep well
   c. concentrate better

7. Calories that have no nutritional value are called _____ calories.
   a. dead
   b. empty
   c. useless

8. Drinking soda can make you feel _____.
   a. happier
   b. more tired
   c. hungrier

9. Dark chocolate _____.
   a. is good for your heart
   b. has less fat than milk chocolate
   c. can increase your blood pressure

D. **Mark these statements *T* (true) or *F* (false). Then write a sentence to explain why, using the information from Listening 1 to support your answers.**

____ 1.   It is important to know what effects food and drink have on our bodies.

_____

T 2. Eating lots of fruits and vegetables is essential to a healthy diet.

_____

F 3. Red meat is just as healthy as white meat.

_____

____ 4. It is better to avoid drinking coffee.

_____

T 5. It is OK to consume things we know are bad for us.

_____

iQ ONLINE **E.** Go online to listen to *Governing What We Eat* and check your comprehension.

F. VOCABULARY Use the new vocabulary from Listening 1. Complete each sentence with the correct word from the list.

mix *(v.)*	rely on *(phr. v.)*	calories *(n.)*	mood *(n.)*	concentrate *(v.)*
spicy *(adj.)*	consume *(v.)*	diet *(n.)*	wise *(adj.)*	balanced *(adj.)*

1. My _____diet_____ includes a lot of chicken and rice.

2. If you __consume__ too much food, you will gain weight.

3. I can't cook, so I __rely on__ my mother to make my meals.

4. I'm not going to eat this candy bar because it has 450 __calories__.

5. I love chocolate because it always puts me in a good __mood__.

6. I can't eat ___spicy___ food because it upsets my stomach.

7. Do you think it's __wise__ to go jogging right after a big meal?

8. According to the recipe, you have to __mix__ the flour and sugar together before adding the eggs.

9. Please don't talk to me while I'm cooking. I need to __concentrate__.

10. A good way to stay healthy is to eat __balanced__ meals and exercise regularly.

iQ ONLINE **G.** Go online for more practice with the vocabulary.

Q SAY WHAT YOU THINK

Discuss the questions in a group.

1. Do you agree with Dr. O'Ryan's advice for a healthy diet? Why or why not?

2. Do you think people worry too much about nutrition? Give examples.

3. Do you agree that "you are what you eat"?

Listening Skill	Listening for causes and effects

Speakers often talk about **causes** and **effects** to help explain their opinions. Listening for the linking words and phrases that connect causes (reasons) and effects (results) will help you understand a speaker's main points.

Here are some words and phrases that signal causes and effects.

I rarely cook **because** I am tired when I get home.
effect — cause

We usually eat at home **since** it's so expensive to eat out these days.
effect — cause

I never buy fish **as** I don't know how to cook it.
effect — cause

The pasta tasted terrible, **so** we didn't eat it.
cause — effect

Due to her healthy diet, Keiko lived to be 110 years old.
cause — effect

Because of the high calories, I never eat chocolate.
cause — effect

Note: Use *due to* and *because of* before noun phrases. Use *because, since, as,* and *so* before clauses.

A. Listen to the sentences. Complete each sentence with the correct word or phrase.

1. _____Since_____ Dr. O'Ryan is a nutrition expert, Andy interviewed her on his radio show.

2. Eating a lot of cheese isn't good _____because_____ the large amount of salt.

3. _____because_____ Andy stopped drinking soda, he feels much healthier now.

4. Andy also wants to lose weight, _____so_____ he's following Dr. O'Ryan's suggestions.

B. Listen to four statements from the radio show. Complete the chart with the causes or effects you hear. Then circle the linking words.

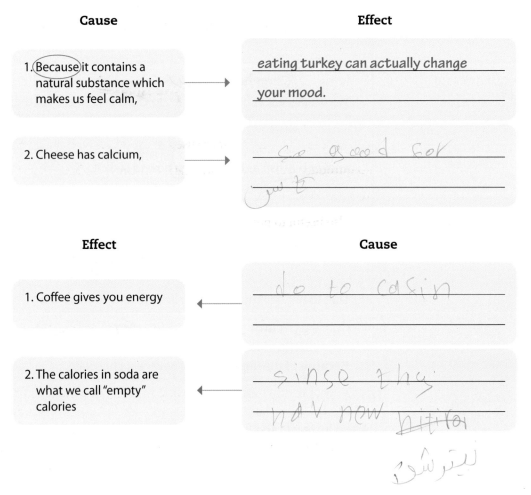

Cause	Effect
1. (Because) it contains a natural substance which makes us feel calm,	eating turkey can actually change your mood.
2. Cheese has calcium,	_so is good for_ _____

Effect	Cause
1. Coffee gives you energy	_do to cafin_
2. The calories in soda are what we call "empty" calories	_since the_ _nav new_

بيترشدو

C. Think about your diet. How does what you eat affect you? For example, does it make you feel tired or awake, nervous or happy? Does the time of day make a difference? Make notes and share your ideas with a partner. Be sure to use linking words and phrases when giving causes and effects.

I never eat ice cream because it makes my teeth hurt.

Sometimes I drink coffee in the morning as it helps to wake me up.

iQ ONLINE **D.** Go online for more practice with listening for causes and effects.

Note-taking Skill | **Taking notes on causes and effects**

When listening to identify causes and effects, you need to listen carefully for the key words and phrases that are used to introduce both causes and their effects.

To introduce a cause, you may hear: *as, because, because of, due to, since*

To introduce an effect, you may hear: *as a result, consequently, so, therefore*

It is also useful to prepare a T-chart to help you classify the information. Write *Cause* and *Effect* in a T-chart and note each piece of information in the appropriate column as you listen. Organizing your notes in this way will help you understand how the ideas relate to one another. It will also make it easier to review your notes.

A. Read this section of a talk on nutrition. Circle the words that introduce causes and effects.

Fast food is more popular today than ever before. Because of our busy lifestyle, people don't always have time to cook their own meals. It may be more expensive than cooking for yourself, but every day millions of us choose a pizza or take-out instead of a home-cooked meal. The downside is that although fast food is quick and easy, it is expensive, so it can be bad for our wallets. What's more, it is bad for our health, too, as a lot of fast food contains high levels of sugar and salt. Also, it is easy to eat too much due to special promotions that encourage us to buy more than we need. For all these reasons, we need to start making healthier food choices.

B. Use this T-chart to complete each cause and effect.

Cause	Effect
1. busy lifestyle	*no time to cook it can be bad for our wallet*
2. it is expensive	
3. _____	bad for health
4. _____	eat too much

 **C.** Go online for more practice taking notes on causes and effects.

LISTENING 2 | Food Tasters

UNIT OBJECTIVE ▶▶▶▶ You are going to listen to some lectures from a career website. Three professional food tasters talk about their jobs. As you listen, gather information and ideas about the importance of taste and nutrition.

PREVIEW THE LISTENING

A. PREVIEW What skills do you think a food taster needs to have? Do you think this job requires training? What kinds of foods do you think a food taster might taste?

cheese

chocolate

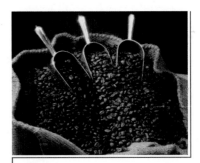
coffee

iQ ONLINE

VOCABULARY Read aloud these words from Listening 2. Check (✓) the ones you know. Use a dictionary to find the meaning of any words you do not know. Then discuss with a partner how these words may relate to the unit.

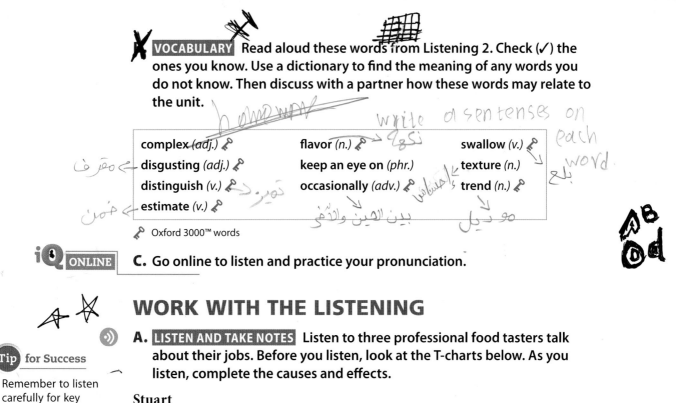

complex *(adj.)* 🗝	flavor *(n.)* 🗝	swallow *(v.)* 🗝
disgusting *(adj.)* 🗝	keep an eye on *(phr.)*	texture *(n.)* 🗝
distinguish *(v.)* 🗝	occasionally *(adv.)* 🗝	trend *(n.)* 🗝
estimate *(v.)* 🗝		

🗝 Oxford 3000™ words

C. Go online to listen and practice your pronunciation.

WORK WITH THE LISTENING

A. **LISTEN AND TAKE NOTES** Listen to three professional food tasters talk about their jobs. Before you listen, look at the T-charts below. As you listen, complete the causes and effects.

Tip for Success

Remember to listen carefully for key words that introduce causes and effects.

Stuart

Cause	Effect
loves chocolate	this is his _____
everybody _____	volunteers easy to find
easy to put on weight	tries to _____
has to keep up with _____	travels a lot

Marie

Cause	Effect
all taste different	need to _____
keep cheeses for a long time	has to decide _____
need to _____	convenient to live outside Paris
people like to try _____	must develop new products

Enrique

Cause	Effect
sense of taste best in mornings	only _____
people pay a lot for coffee	want to _____
tastes up to 100 coffees	doesn't _____
lives _____	walks to work

Stuart …

T 1. has a degree in nutrition.

F 2. started this job immediately after graduation.

F 3. visits the dentist once a year.   6 months

Marie …

F 4. doesn't like strong-smelling cheeses.

___ 5. often visits local farmers.

T 6. has a degree in food science.

◗)) **C.** Listen again to Enrique. Circle the answer that best completes each statement.

1. Enrique started work as a (manager / waiter) in a coffee shop.

2. He (has / does not have) a professional qualification.

3. He works for a large (importing / exporting) company.

4. He checks the (price / quality) of the coffee.

5. In the afternoons he (emails clients / contacts suppliers).

D. Read these summaries. Work with a partner to find two mistakes in each one. Correct the mistakes.

1. Stuart is a chocolate taster for an ice cream manufacturer. He has a degree in nutrition. He trains staff, visits factories, and deals with suppliers. He has worked in his current job for eight years. He likes to keep fit and eat healthily.

2. Marie is a cheese buyer for a large supermarket. On a taste day, she checks the flavor, texture, and smell of up to 10 different cheeses. She especially likes strong-smelling cheeses. She sometimes gets tired of her job.

3. Enrique works as a trainee coffee taster. He checks the quality of coffee, its smell and taste, and how sweet or bitter it is. He loves his job. To him, trying to tell the differences between different coffees is very easy.

Vocabulary
Skill Review

In Unit 1 you learned about suffixes. Review the common suffixes on page 17. Notice how these suffixes can help you identify the correct part of speech.

E. **VOCABULARY** Use the new vocabulary from Listening 2. Read the sentences. Circle the answer that best matches the meaning of each bold word or phrase.

1. Some of the best dishes are made with a variety of spices. This gives them a **complex** flavor.
   a. complicated   b. uninteresting   c. important

2. That cheese smells **disgusting**. Throw it away!
   a. disappointing   b. amazing   c. terrible

3. Hold your nose and close your eyes, and you'll find it hard to **distinguish** between an onion and an apple.
   a. see   b. know   c. tell the difference

4. Scientists don't exactly know, but they **estimate** that 80 percent of what we taste is due to smell.
   a. promise   b. agree completely   c. calculate approximately

5. Children often don't like to eat food with strong **flavors**, but they grow to like them as they get older.
   a. senses   b. tastes   c. feelings

6. Could you **keep an eye on** the cookies in the oven while I'm out? I don't want them to burn.
   a. think about   b. listen to   c. check often

7. I don't eat eggs much, but **occasionally** I have an omelet.
   a. frequently   b. never   c. sometimes

8. You should **swallow** your vitamins with a full glass of water.
   a. try   b. take   c. mix

9. I don't like the **texture** of this bread—it's too hard for me.
   a. feel   b. look   c. taste

10. I don't take dieting **trends** seriously since they change so often.
    a. fashions   b. meals   c. restaurants

iQ ONLINE   **F.** Go online for more practice with the vocabulary.

SAY WHAT YOU THINK

A. Discuss the questions in a group.

1. Which do you like best: chocolate, cheese, or coffee? Why do you like it so much?

2. Do you think you might like to be a food taster? Why or why not?

B. Before you watch the video, discuss the questions in a group.

1. What kinds of foods contain carbohydrates? Is it better to eat before or after exercise?

2. How can food help the brain? Are some foods better for the brain than others? Does it really matter what time of day you eat?

iQ ONLINE

C. Go online to watch a video about food and the body and brain. Then check your comprehension.

D. Think about the unit video, Listening 1, and Listening 2 as you discuss the questions.

1. In what ways can what we eat affect our health and well-being? How healthy is your diet and lifestyle?

2. Who is most responsible for making sure we make the right food choices: the government, parents, teachers, or ourselves? How can people who eat unhealthy food be encouraged to change their habits?

Collocations are combinations of words that are often used together. For example, certain adjectives go together with certain nouns. Using correct collocations will make your conversations sound more natural.

Here are some examples of adjective-noun collocations.

> When you eat before exercising, you should only have a **light meal**.
> There is nothing better than a **cold drink** on a hot summer day.
> I try not to eat too much **fast food**, but it's difficult because I love fries.
> Would you like cheesecake for dessert or just some **fresh fruit**?

A. Complete each collocation with a noun from the box.

diet	drink	food	snack	steak

1. a soft _____

2. junk _____

3. a juicy _____

4. a balanced _____

5. a quick _____

B. Complete each sentence with the correct collocation from Activity A.

1. Jim's favorite meal to cook at home is _____,
   served with potatoes.

2. To have _____, you need to eat lots of different
   kinds of foods.

3. Do you want tea, or would you like _____
   with lunch?

4. I used to eat chips and candy all the time. Now I hate _____!

5. I don't have time for a big lunch, so let's just have _____.

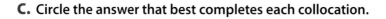

C. Circle the answer that best completes each collocation.

1. James has always had a very _____ appetite.
    a. healthy
    b. fit

2. Generally, I try to avoid eating a lot of fatty _____.
    a. cooking
    b. foods

3. Is all the fish on the menu deep _____?
    a. grilled
    b. fried

4. _____ exercise is an important part of staying healthy.
    a. Regular
    b. Steady

5. I like cooking, but I hate washing all the _____ dishes afterwards.
    a. filthy
    b. dirty

iQ ONLINE **D.** Go online for more practice with adjective-noun collocations.

 **UNIT OBJECTIVE** ▶▶▶▶ At the end of this unit, you will interview three classmates about their favorite dishes. Make sure to give advice when you conduct your interviews.

Grammar	Quantifiers with count/noncount nouns

Count nouns are the names of things we can count, for example, one egg and two bananas. **Noncount nouns** are the names of things we cannot count, such as cheese and water.

how many/how much

Use *how many* with count nouns. Use *how much* with noncount nouns.

> **How many** apples do you eat a week?
> **How much** tea do you drink a day?

too many/too much

Use *too many/too much* when there is more than you want or need.

> You can have cookies once in a while, but don't eat **too many**.
> Don't drink **too much** coffee at bedtime, or you'll never fall asleep.

enough/not enough

Use *enough/not enough* with both count and noncount nouns.

> We have **enough** food for everybody.
> We don't have **enough** chairs.

chilies

A. Complete the conversations with words and phrases from the box. Then practice the conversations with a partner.

enough	many	too many
not enough	much	too much

Eileen: Hey, that smells great. What are you cooking?

Debra: Chicken with chilies and rice. Do you want to try some?

Eileen: Sure … Wow! That's hot! How __enough__ chilies did you put in?
                                                              1

Debra: Five. But they're really small. Don't you like spicy food?

Eileen: Yeah, I do, but it's too hot for me!

Anna: What do you think of the soup? It's potato and onion.

Susie: Hmm. It's OK. It seems like there is something missing, though.

Anna: Maybe I didn't put in _to mem_ salt.
₂

Susie: And it's pretty thick, isn't it?

Anna: Yes. I think I used _to much_ potatoes.
₃

Muriel: How _mamy_ sugar did you put in this coffee?
₄

Angela: One teaspoon.

Muriel: That's _not enoubt_ for me! I like my coffee very sweet.
₅

Angela: Well, you shouldn't have _enooht_. You'll get fat.
₆

B. Make a list of foods and drinks you like. Write *C* (count) or *N* (noncount) next to each item. Then discuss your favorite things to eat and drink with a partner. Be sure to use *much*, *many*, and *enough* correctly with count and noncount nouns.

Foods I like …   Drinks I like …

sechy _____   _____

boln _____   _____

Homos _____   _____

C. Go online for more practice using quantifiers with count and noncount nouns.

D. Go online for the grammar expansion.

When certain words follow each other, additional sounds are created. These extra sounds make a natural **link** between the two words.

When a word beginning with a vowel follows a word that ends in the vowel sounds /i/, /eɪ/, or /aɪ/ (like *bee, say,* or *eye*), a /j/ sound is added between the words.

> I think Marco must **be** /j/ **Italian.**
> I can't see you tonight, but Tues**day** /j/ **is** fine.
> **I** /j/ **ate** salmon for dinner last night.

When a word beginning with a vowel follows a word that ends in the vowel sounds /u/, /o/, or /aʊ/ (like *who, no* and *how*), a /w/ sound is added between the words.

> Do **you** /w/ **eat** a balanced diet?
> Do you want to **go** /w/ **out** for lunch?
> **How** /w/ **is** your steak?

Pronouncing these linking sounds will help make your English sound more natural.

A. Listen to the sentences. Write /j/ or /w/ in the correct places. Then listen again and check your answers.

1. We /j/ all   eat   things   we   know   we   shouldn't.

2. "Empty"   calories   have   no   nutritional   value   at   all.

3. I   can't   drink   coffee,   but   tea   is   fine.

4. Cheese   has   calcium,   so   it's   good   for   your   teeth.

5. Sometimes   in   the   evening   I'm   too   tired   to   cook.

6. Marie   makes   sure   the   cheese   is   ready   to   go   out   on   sale.

7. Stuart   thinks   the   appearance   of   chocolate   can   be   as   important   as   the   taste.

8. Enrique   thinks   people   pay   a   lot   for   coffee   so   they   want   to   enjoy   it.

B. Listen again. Repeat each sentence. Practice linking /j/ and /w/.

C. Go online for more practice using links with /j/ and /w/.

The words *should*, *shouldn't*, and *ought to* are used to give advice. Listen to these sentences.

> According to Dr. O'Ryan, Andy **should** drink less coffee.
> He **shouldn't** drink a lot of soda.
> He **ought to** eat more fish.

You can sound more polite by starting a sentence with *perhaps*.

> **Perhaps** you **should** eat more fruit and vegetables.

You can give stronger advice by adding *really*.

> You **really ought to** eat more fruit and vegetables.

A. Work with a partner. Discuss your eating and drinking habits. Take turns making true statements about your diet. After each of your partner's statements, give some advice, using *should/shouldn't* or *ought to*. Remember to use count/noncount nouns correctly.

A: *I probably eat too much fast food.*

B: *You should try to eat more healthily. For example, you shouldn't eat fries for lunch. Perhaps you should eat a salad instead.*

B. Think about the advice your partner gave you. Work in a group. Share the advice you received.

I eat too much fast food, so I should try to eat more healthily. For example, I ought to eat a salad for lunch instead of fries.

iQ ONLINE   **C.** Go online for more practice giving advice.

UNIT OBJECTIVE ▶▶▶ In this assignment, you are going to interview three classmates about their favorite dishes. As you prepare your interview, think about the Unit Question, "What's more important: taste or nutrition?" Use information from Listening 1, Listening 2, the unit video, and your work in this unit to support your interview. Refer to the Self-Assessment checklist on page 50.

CONSIDER THE IDEAS

Work in a group. Match each dish with the country it comes from. Then discuss which dishes you have tried and whether or not you liked them.

____ 1. fondue   a. Japan

____ 2. pizza   b. Saudi Arabia

____ 3. kabsa   c. Switzerland

____ 4. moussaka   d. Greece

____ 5. sushi   e. Mexico

____ 6. tacos   f. Italy

fondue

What other dishes from around the world do you know? In your group, quiz each other on where different dishes come from.

A: *Where does paella come from?*
B: *Uh … Spain!*

Paella Valenciana

PREPARE AND SPEAK

A. **GATHER IDEAS** Make a list of your favorite dishes, either from your own country or from other cultures.

kbala

shawrma

Taimiah

B. **ORGANIZE IDEAS** Choose one dish from your list in Activity A. Use the outline to help you prepare to talk about it. Do not write exactly what you are going to say. Just write notes to help you organize your ideas.

MY FAVORITE DISH

What's the name of the dish?

_____

Where is it from? _____

What are the ingredients? _____

_____

How healthy is this dish? _____

Why do you particularly like this dish? _you can_
have it cheken amd beef and
you but it
_____

Tip for Success

When making notes, don't write full sentences. Just write the important words.

C. **SPEAK** Complete these steps. Refer to the Self-Assessment checklist on page 50 before you begin.

1. Interview three students.

2. Ask them about their favorite dishes from Activity B, and take notes in the chart.

3. When you talk about your own favorite dish, use your notes from Activity B to help you. Do not read exactly what you wrote; just use your notes.

	Classmate 1	Classmate 2	Classmate 3
Dish			
Country			
Ingredients			
Is it healthy?			
Reasons for liking it?			

4. When you finish, discuss your interviews in a group. Do more of your classmates choose their favorite dish because of taste or nutrition? Whose favorite dish would you like to try?

 Go online for your alternate Unit Assignment.

CHECK AND REFLECT

A. CHECK Think about the Unit Assignment as you complete the Self-Assessment checklist.

Yes	No	SELF-ASSESSMENT
☐	☐	I was able to speak easily about the topic.
☐	☐	My classmates understood me.
☐	☐	I used vocabulary from the unit.
☐	☐	I used quantifiers with count/noncount nouns.
☐	☐	I used links with /j/ and /w/.
☐	☐	I gave advice.

B. REFLECT Go to the Online Discussion Board to discuss these questions.

1. What is something new you learned in this unit?

2. Look back at the Unit Question—What's more important: taste or nutrition? Is your answer different now than when you started this unit? If yes, how is it different? Why?

collictions (handwritten)

TRACK YOUR SUCCESS

Circle the words and phrases you have learned in this unit.

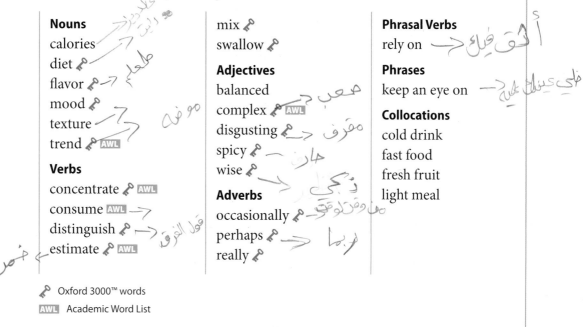

Nouns
calories
diet
flavor
mood
texture
trend AWL

Verbs
concentrate AWL
consume AWL
distinguish
estimate AWL

mix
swallow

Adjectives
balanced
complex AWL
disgusting
spicy
wise

Adverbs
occasionally
perhaps
really

Phrasal Verbs
rely on

Phrases
keep an eye on

Collocations
cold drink
fast food
fresh fruit
light meal

Oxford 3000™ words
AWL Academic Word List

Check (✓) the skills you learned. If you need more work on a skill, refer to the page(s) in parentheses.

LISTENING ☐	I can listen for causes and effects. (p. 33)
NOTE TAKING ☐	I can take notes on causes and effects (p. 35)
VOCABULARY ☐	I can use adjective-noun collocations. (p. 41)
GRAMMAR ☐	I can use quantifiers with count/noncount nouns. (p. 43)
PRONUNCIATION ☐	I can link words with /j/ and /w/ sounds. (p. 45)
SPEAKING ☐	I can give advice. (p. 46)
UNIT OBJECTIVE ▶▶▶▶ ☐	I can gather information and ideas to conduct a class survey on food preferences.

UNIT 3

Psychology

NOTE TAKING	▶	taking notes on advantages and disadvantages
LISTENING	▶	listening for time markers
VOCABULARY	▶	using the dictionary
GRAMMAR	▶	tag questions
PRONUNCIATION	▶	intonation in tag questions
SPEAKING	▶	asking for and giving reasons

UNIT QUESTION

Is change good or bad?

A Discuss these questions with your classmates.

1. What has been the biggest change in your life recently? How did it affect you?

2. Is there anything in your life right now that you would like to change?

3. Look at the photo. What kind of change is taking place? Would you ever make this kind of change in your life? How?

B Listen to *The Q Classroom* online. Then answer these questions.

1. Felix thinks that most changes have a good and a bad side. Do you agree? Can you think of any examples?

2. Yuna says she is happy about starting school full time. How did you feel when you began your course here? How did your life change as a result?

iQ ONLINE **C** Go to the Online Discussion Board to discuss the Unit Question with your classmates.

OVERSIZE LOAD

D Complete the questionnaire.

HOW DO YOU FEEL ABOUT Change?

1 When I go on vacation, I prefer to…

a. go to the same place every year.
b. go somewhere different each time.

2 When I watch TV, I…

a. watch the same programs every week.
b. try to find something new to watch.

3 When I go shopping for food, I usually…

a. buy the same things.
b. look for something different.

4 The idea of moving to a different city makes me feel…

a. worried.
b. excited.

5 When it's time to have my hair cut, I prefer to…

a. keep the same hairstyle.
b. try a different look if I feel like it.

6 In my future career, I think I will…

a. have the same job my whole life.
b. try a few different jobs.

7 When it comes to my TV, cell phone, and camera, I usually…

a. keep them until they break.
b. replace them when I want to.

8 When I buy new clothes, I usually…

a. choose the same style and color.
b. look for something in the latest fashion.

How well did you do?

If you chose *a* for most of your answers, you prefer things to stay the same, and perhaps feel fairly cautious about change. You know what you like, so trying new things worries you. Don't be afraid to take a few chances from time to time—you might enjoy something different.

If you chose *b* for most of your answers, you are happy to try new experiences and are open to new ideas. You love variety, but be careful—you don't need to change everything all the time! Perhaps you should think more carefully before you decide to change things.

If you chose *a* and *b* equally, you are very balanced. You welcome change sometimes, but you don't want things to change all the time. Congratulations!

E Discuss your answers in a group. Do you think the questionnaire is accurate? Why or why not? Use examples from your own life to support your opinion.

Using a T-chart is a simple way to separate information when you take notes. You can use a T-chart to help you see two sides of an argument, the advantages and disadvantages of a topic, or the strengths and weaknesses of an idea.

When someone is giving their opinion on a subject, you can use a T-chart to separate their opinions when you take notes. Simply write *Advantages* and *Disadvantages* in a T-chart and note each opinion in the appropriate column as you listen. This will help you understand the opposing viewpoints more clearly.

A. Read this section of a talk on the impact of the Internet. Underline the opinions in favor of and against the Internet.

The Internet has profoundly changed the way we live. Unlike traditional mail, we can communicate instantly with people anywhere in the world. We can keep in touch with family and friends. Companies can promote their products and services 24 hours a day via websites. We can also find information on almost any topic and access a wide range of entertainment; we can play games, watch movies, etc. However, some people say the Internet can harm relationships as it replaces face-to-face communication with a virtual world. Other drawbacks include unwanted emails (spam), viruses, which can damage your computer, and spyware that steals your personal information. Not everyone welcomes the changes that the Internet has brought.

B. Note each advantage and disadvantage in the T-chart.

Critical Thinking **Tip**

In Activity B, you use a T-chart to **summarize** the advantages and disadvantages of the Internet. When you summarize, you give the main points but not all the details.

Advantages	Disadvantages

C. Work with a partner. Discuss the advantages and disadvantages of the Internet. Use your T-chart from Activity B to help you.

D. Go online for more practice taking notes on advantages and disadvantages.

LISTENING

LISTENING 1 | Changing Expectations

UNIT OBJECTIVE ▶▶▶▶ You are going to listen to Gary McBride talk about how his life has changed after leaving a high-paying job on Wall Street to work in a small town in Iowa. As you listen to the talk, gather information and ideas about the advantages and disadvantages of change.

PREVIEW THE LISTENING

A. PREVIEW Why do you think Gary wanted to do something different? Check (✓) your predictions.

☐ He was bored with his job.

☐ He wanted to travel around the world.

☐ He decided to start his own business.

☐ He wanted to spend more time with his family.

Gary McBride

B. VOCABULARY Read aloud these words from Listening 1. Check (✓) the ones you know. Use a dictionary to define any new or unknown words. Then discuss with a partner how the words will relate to Gary's story.

تأقلم ←

راضي ←

يعني أقو ها عشان تسويه ←
يصرف الورقة
كذلك
نفس كائن لا

adapt (v.) 🔑	handle (v.) 🔑
considerably (adv.) 🔑	justify (v.) 🔑
crisis (n.) 🔑	position (n.) 🔑
curious (adj.) 🔑	steady (adj.) 🔑
fulfilled (adj.)	suffer (v.) 🔑

يتألم

🔑 Oxford 3000™ words

iQ ONLINE **C.** Go online to listen and practice your pronunciation.

good salris

con't hed
pesnal Lifo
qurids
relishoship

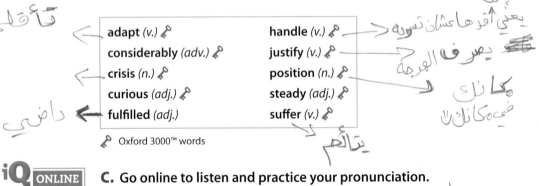

WORK WITH THE LISTENING

A. **LISTEN AND TAKE NOTES** Listen to an excerpt from Gary's talk. He is talking about his life as a city trader. As you listen, take notes in the T-chart on the advantages and disadvantages he mentions.

Tip for Success

Using a **T-chart** is a simple way to separate information when you take notes.

Life as a city trader	
Advantages	**Disadvantages**
very well paid	

B. Now listen to another excerpt from Gary's talk. Here, he is talking about his life as a home-care assistant. As you listen, take notes in the T-chart on the advantages and disadvantages he mentions.

Life as a home-care assistant	
Advantages	**Disadvantages**
Load hospital dower ddapt cvinds mealtour family	New car solde pavement Lover

C. Read the questions. Then listen again to the whole talk. Circle the best answer for each question.

1. Why did Gary stop working as a city trader?
   a. He lost his job.
   b. He became ill.
   c. He couldn't handle the stress.

2. What did Gary do as soon as he left his job?
   a. He looked for another job.
   b. He traveled.
   c. He moved back home.

3. Why did Gary move to Iowa?
   a. He wanted to be near his parents.
   b. He needed to find a better job.
   c. He had some good friends there.

4. How does Gary feel about his new job?

   a. It's very fulfilling.

   b. It can be difficult.

   c. The salary is too low.

5. What goal has Gary achieved?

   a. He has more time to think.

   b. He is happy.

   c. He enjoys his free time.

D. **Read these statements. Write *T* (true) or *F* (false). Then correct the false statements.**

T 1. According to Gary, many people consider "downshifting" at some point in their lives.

_____

F 2. After finishing work as a city trader, he decided to retrain before looking for a new career.

   _____retiring_____

F 3. He was unemployed for six months.   ᵗᵒ(

   _____

F 4. He rejected several job offers before starting work again.

   _____

____ 5. These days he feels he is a better person.

   _____

 E. **Go online to listen to *Change and Stress* and check your comprehension.**

F. VOCABULARY **Use the new vocabulary from Listening 1. Read the sentences. Then match each bold word with its definition below.**

C 1. When the economic **crisis** started, people were suddenly worried about losing their jobs.

E 2. Tina couldn't **handle** all the noise and pollution of living in a city, so she moved to the country.

3. When Brian left his small village to live in the city, it took him a few months to **adapt**.

___ 4. We're **curious** about what it would be like to live in another country. It sounds very interesting.

___ 5. Over the years, Steve's company has developed **steady** and reliable relationships with many other businesses in the area.

___ 6. I felt **fulfilled** as a teacher because I enjoyed helping people learn.

___ 7. There were more than 30 applications for the **position** of general manager.

___ 8. Don't you agree that keeping things the same is **considerably** easier than trying to change them?

___ 9. After I borrowed money from my parents, I had to **justify** the purchases I made with it.

___ 10. If you focus too much on your job, your personal relationships may **suffer** as a result.

a. *(v.)* to change your behavior because the situation you are in has changed
b. *(adv.)* a lot
c. *(n.)* a time of great danger or difficulty
d. *(adj.)* wanting to know or learn something
e. *(adj.)* completely satisfied and happy
f. *(v.)* to control or deal with someone or something
g. *(v.)* to give or be a good reason for something
h. *(n.)* a job
i. *(adj.)* staying the same over a period of time
j. *(v.)* to become worse in quality

 G. Go online for more practice with the vocabulary.

SAY WHAT YOU THINK

Discuss the questions in a group.

1. What did Gary learn by changing his career? Do you think the lesson will last?

2. What benefits from his old job might Gary miss?

3. Do you think you could change your life completely in this way? Why or why not?

When listening to a narrative, such as someone telling a story, it can be useful to listen for time markers. Time markers help to establish when something happened, for how long, etc. By listening for time markers, you can more easily understand past events and how they relate to one another. Here are some words and phrases that are commonly used as time markers.

> now/nowadays
> before/after
> then, next, after that
> three days **ago**
> **for** two weeks
> these days

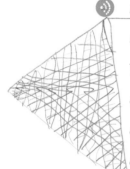

A. Listen again to Gary's talk. Match each time marker (a–e) with an event (1–5).

a. A few years ago   1. the financial crisis came along.

b. Then   2. I'm still a home-care assistant.

c. For six months   3. I started looking for work.

d. After a couple of months   4. I worked on Wall Street.

e. These days   5. I traveled around the world.

B. Think about an important change that happened in your life. Make notes, using time markers to help clarify what happened and when.

C. Work with a partner. Discuss the important change in your life, using the notes you made in Activity B. Make sure you use time markers to help your partner understand.

D. Go online for more practice listening for time markers.

UNIT OBJECTIVE ▶▶▶▶ You are going to listen to a radio interview with Barbara Ehrenreich, a well-known journalist and author. As you listen to the interview, gather information and ideas about the advantages and disadvantages of change.

PREVIEW THE LISTENING

Barbara Ehrenreich

A. PREVIEW Why do you think a journalist might decide to "go undercover" to do research? Discuss your ideas with a partner.

B. VOCABULARY Read aloud these words from Listening 2. Check (✓) the ones you know. Use a dictionary to define any new or unknown words. Then discuss with a partner how the words will relate to the unit.

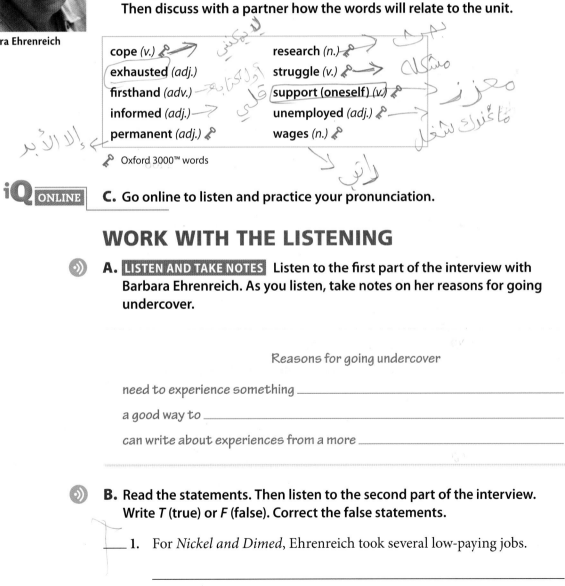

cope (v.) 🔑	research (n.) 🔑
exhausted (adj.)	struggle (v.) 🔑
firsthand (adv.)	support (oneself) (v.) 🔑
informed (adj.)	unemployed (adj.) 🔑
permanent (adj.) 🔑	wages (n.) 🔑

🔑 Oxford 3000™ words

iQ ONLINE **C.** Go online to listen and practice your pronunciation.

WORK WITH THE LISTENING

A. LISTEN AND TAKE NOTES Listen to the first part of the interview with Barbara Ehrenreich. As you listen, take notes on her reasons for going undercover.

> Reasons for going undercover
>
> need to experience something _____
>
> a good way to _____
>
> can write about experiences from a more _____

B. Read the statements. Then listen to the second part of the interview. Write *T* (true) or *F* (false). Correct the false statements.

____ 1. For *Nickel and Dimed*, Ehrenreich took several low-paying jobs.

_____

2. Ehrenreich found that it wasn't so difficult to cope financially.

_____

3. For *Bait and Switch*, Ehrenreich researched unemployment among white-collar workers.

_____

4. Ehrenreich found that life was more difficult for white-collar workers than unskilled workers.

_____

5. Ehrenreich is pleased that the changes she made were temporary.

_____

6. Ehrenreich didn't learn as much as she expected by going undercover.

_____

 C. Read the statements. Then listen again. Circle the answer that best completes each statement.

1. For her book *Nickel and Dimed*, Ehrenreich worked undercover in each job for _____.
   a. one month
   b. three months
   c. six months

2. While Ehrenreich was working undercover, _____.
   a. she studied hard
   b. she had a lot of fun
   c. her life changed completely

3. Ehrenreich found that it was difficult to manage financially because _____ were so high.
   a. food prices
   b. travel expenses
   c. rents

4. Ehrenreich says that some of the jobs made her feel _____.
   a. very tired
   b. very bored
   c. very angry

5. Ehrenreich didn't expect *Nickel and Dimed* to be so _____.

    a. expensive

    b. popular

    c. easy to write

6. For her next book, *Bait and Switch*, Ehrenreich _____.

    a. used a false name

    b. took several top jobs

    c. didn't do any research

7. For *Bait and Switch*, Ehrenreich pretended to be an unemployed _____ executive.

    a. account

    b. human resources

    c. public relations

8. Even though Ehrenreich claimed to have _____, she couldn't find any work.

    a. letters of recommendation

    b. a lot of experience

    c. great qualifications

D. Work with a partner. Take notes on each book. In what ways are they similar? In what ways are they different?

Book	Notes
Nickel and Dimed	
Bait and Switch	

Vocabulary
Skill Review

In Unit 2, you learned about adjective-noun collocations. Can you find any adjective-noun collocations in Activity E? Underline them.

E. **VOCABULARY** Use the new vocabulary from Listening 2. Read the sentences. Circle the answer that best matches the meaning of each bold word or phrase.

1. It can be very difficult for people working in low-paying jobs to **cope**.

    a. manage financially

    b. build relationships

    c. be happy

2. After working for ten hours without a break, we were **exhausted**.

    a. very excited

    b. very bored

    c. very tired

3. It's hard to truly understand someone else's situation. Sometimes you need to experience it **firsthand**.
   a. quickly
   b. directly
   c. together

4. You need to know all the facts before you can make an **informed** decision.
   a. detailed
   b. serious
   c. educated

5. Agostino is always happy. He has a **permanent** smile on his face.
   a. constant → for ever
   b. occasional
   c. attractive

6. Sociologists are doing **research** on how people live in the poorest parts of the city.
   a. estimates
   b. practice
   c. studies

7. Many people who don't have jobs **struggle** when it is time to pay their bills.
   a. work hard
   b. have difficulty
   c. invest money

8. Many students at college don't receive money from their parents. They need to be able to **support themselves**.
   a. take care of themselves
   b. live together
   c. enjoy themselves

9. When the company closed down, many of its workers became **unemployed**.
   a. jobless
   b. educated
   c. sick

10. I enjoy my work, but the **wages** are too low for me to make a living.
    a. benefits
    b. earnings
    c. conditions

F. Go online for more practice with the vocabulary.

 # SAY WHAT YOU THINK

A. Discuss the questions in a group.

1. Why do you think *Nickel and Dimed* was a best seller?

2. What qualities do you think a person needs to go undercover as Ehrenreich did? Would you like to try doing this? Why or why not?

> **Tip for Success**
>
> Be an active listener! Use expressions such as *Really?, Hmm, Yeah,* and *I see* to show that you are paying attention to the speaker.

B. Before you watch the video, discuss these questions in a group.

1. How easy do you think it is for someone to change careers?

2. What are the challenges in changing to a completely different kind of job? What are the potential benefits?

 C. Go online to watch a video about how Christine Marchuska changed her life after losing her job on Wall Street. Then check your comprehension.

> **VIDEO VOCABULARY**
>
> **burned-out** *(adj.)* feeling as if you have done something too long and need a rest
>
> **ecstatic** *(adj.)* very happy, excited, and enthusiastic
>
> **head back** *(v.)* return
>
> **Ivy League** *(n.)* a group of eight universities in the United States with high academic standards, a prestigious social status, and long-standing traditions
>
> **philanthropy** *(n.)* the practice of helping the poor and those in need

D. Think about the unit video, Listening 1, and Listening 2 as you discuss these questions.

1. Think about the changes that Gary McBride and Barbara Ehrenreich experienced. How were their experiences similar? How were they different?

2. What did each person learn from change? Who do you think learned more? Explain your reasons.

A **word web** is a diagram that connects words. You can use a word web to show the different meanings of a word.

- Start with a word with multiple meanings, such as *get*. Write the word in the middle circle of the word web.
- Next, look up the word in the dictionary. Some dictionaries have shortcuts, words that help you find the different meanings more quickly.
- Write each shortcut word in a circle surrounding the middle circle.
- Include an example sentence to help you understand the word and show how it is used in English.

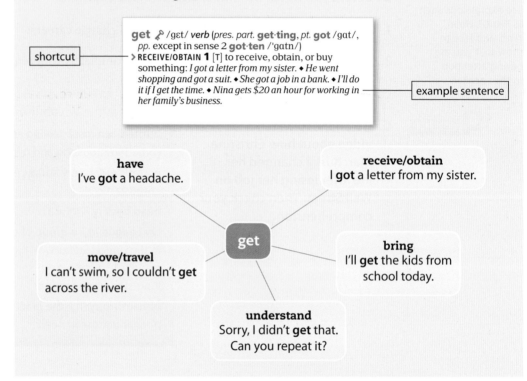

shortcut

get 🔑 /gɛt/ *verb* (*pres. part.* **get·ting**, *pt.* **got** /gɑt/, *pp.* except in sense 2 **got·ten** /ˈgɑtn/)
❯ RECEIVE/OBTAIN **1** [T] to receive, obtain, or buy something: *I got a letter from my sister.* ♦ *He went shopping and got a suit.* ♦ *She got a job in a bank.* ♦ *I'll do it if I get the time.* ♦ *Nina gets $20 an hour for working in her family's business.*

example sentence

have
I've **got** a headache.

receive/obtain
I **got** a letter from my sister.

move/travel
I can't swim, so I couldn't **get** across the river.

get

bring
I'll **get** the kids from school today.

understand
Sorry, I didn't **get** that. Can you repeat it?

All dictionary entries are from the *Oxford American Dictionary for learners of English* © Oxford University Press 2011.

A. Read the sentences. Then write the number of each sentence below the correct shortcut in the word web. Use a dictionary to help you if necessary.

1. This town has changed a lot in recent years.

2. You need to change the light bulb in the kitchen.

3. It's quicker by bus, but you have to change twice.

4. Do you want to change before we go out?

5. Can you change a twenty-dollar bill?

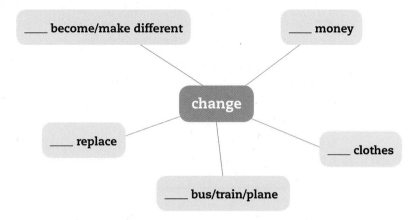

B. Work with a partner. Use a dictionary to help you complete this word web with the verb *make*. Follow the steps in the Vocabulary Skill box.

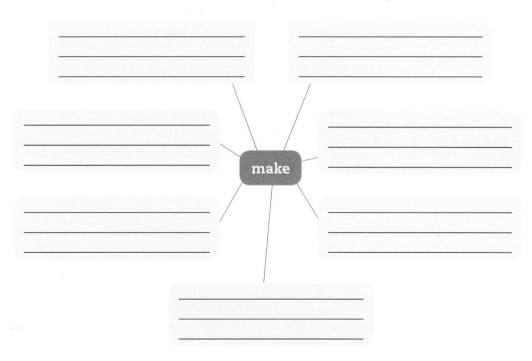

 C. Go online for more practice with using the dictionary.

SPEAKING

At the end of this unit, you will take part in a group discussion about the advantages and disadvantages of change. Make sure you give reasons for your opinions and ask others for their reasons.

Grammar | Tag questions

Tag questions are common in everyday conversation. You can use a tag question to keep a conversation going by asking a person for her opinion about a situation.

Tag questions are formed by adding a short *yes/no* question at the end of a statement.

If the statement is positive, the tag question is negative.

☐ Starting a new job **is** exciting, **isn't it**?

If the statement is negative, the tag question is positive.

☐ They **aren't** moving home, **are they**?

The subject of a tag question is the pronoun form of the subject of the statement.

⌐ **You**'re starting your own business, aren't **you**?
  John went to Australia, didn't **he**?
└ **Your friends** all have jobs, don't **they**?

The verb in a tag question is a form or part of the main verb in the statement.

If the statement contains an auxiliary verb or modal, use the auxiliary verb or modal in the tag question.

⌐ They**'re** curious about the world, **aren't** they?
  All low-paid workers **should** get a raise, **shouldn't** they?
└ You **haven't** told anyone you're leaving, **have** you?

If the statement does not contain an auxiliary verb or modal, use a form of *do* in the tag question.

Your boss **trusts** you, **doesn't** he?
The crisis **got** better, **didn't** it?

A. Use tag questions to complete the conversations. Then practice the conversations with a partner.

1. A: You're a journalist, _____aren't you_____?

   B: Yes, I am.

2. A: Simon never works on the weekend, _____doesn't he_____?

   B: No, he doesn't.

3. A: They got married, _____didn't they_____?

   B: No, they didn't.

4. A: It's important to have good friends, _____isn't it_____?

   B: Yes, it is.

5. A: Susan should see her family more often, _____shouldn't she_____?

   B: Yes, she should.

6. A: Abed and Gary don't have permanent jobs, _____do they_____?

   B: No, they don't.

7. A: Valerie came here from France, _____didn't she_____?

   B: Yes, she did.

8. A: We can't afford an overseas vacation this year, _____can we_____?

   B: Yes, we can!

B. Complete the sentences. Use tag questions. Then add three more sentences with tag questions of your own.

1. You don't like to get your hair cut, _____do you_____?

2. You haven't bought a new cell phone, _____have you_____?

3. You're not thinking of moving abroad, _____are you_____?

4. _____?

5. _____?

6. _____?

C. Work with a partner. Take turns asking and answering the questions from activity B.

D. Go online for more practice with tag questions.

E. Go online for the grammar expansion.

The **intonation** you use in tag questions is very important. Use falling intonation on the tag question when you think you know the answer and you are asking for confirmation. Use rising intonation on the tag question when you are not certain of the answer.

Asking for confirmation

Carol's never worked abroad, has she?   You can scuba dive, can't you?

Uncertain of the answer

Carol's never worked abroad, has she?   You can scuba dive, can't you?

A. Listen to the sentences. Does the intonation rise or fall on each tag question? Check (✓) your answers.

	Rise	Fall
1. You've never been to Europe, have you?	☐	☑
2. Julie and Frank just had a baby, didn't they?	☑	☐
3. You're not looking for a new job, are you?	☐	☑
4. James is retiring next year, isn't he?	☑	☐
5. Kieron moved to New York last year, didn't he?	☐	☑
6. The new housing project was approved, wasn't it?	☑	☐

B. Listen to the sentences. Does the speaker know the answer or not? Check (✓) your answers.

	Knows the answer	Doesn't know the answer
1. You've tried horseback riding, haven't you?	☐	☐
2. Adapting to a new job can be hard, can't it?	☐	☐
3. You wouldn't like to live in New York, would you?	☐	☐
4. You're not afraid of change, are you?	☐	☐
5. Travel is exciting, isn't it?	☐	☐
6. You don't want to work for yourself, do you?	☐	☐

C. Listen again to the sentences from Activities A and B. Repeat the sentences. Use the same intonation that you hear.

D. Work with a partner. Take turns reading the sentences from Activities A and B. Your partner will listen carefully and decide whether your intonation rises or falls.

E. Go online for more practice with intonation in tag questions.

Asking for and giving reasons

To better understand someone's point of view, you can ask the person to explain the **reasons** for his or her opinion. You can also help people understand your point of view by explaining your own reasons. Here are some phrases you can use to ask for or give reasons.

Asking for reasons	Giving reasons
Why do you think/say that?	because …
What are your reasons for saying that?	because of/due to …
Can you explain why …?	The reason … is (that) …
	That's why …

To give several reasons for your point of view, you can introduce each reason with a phrase like these.

First (of all),
Also/Second,
Another reason/thing is …
Finally,

Listen to how the phrases are used in this conversation.

A: You know, I really don't think fishing is for me.
B: Oh yeah? **Why do you say that?**
A: Well, **first of all**, it's boring! **Also**, it's expensive to buy all the equipment, and **another thing** I hate is the smell of fish!

A. Listen to a conversation between two friends. Complete the conversation with the phrases you hear. Then practice the conversation with a partner.

Tip for Success

A good way to keep a conversation going is to ask questions. Asking for more information often helps a conversation become more interesting, too.

Jez: I haven't seen you for ages. How was your vacation in Spain?

Tom: It was great! I tried lots of new things—horseback riding, scuba

diving … I even went to a bullfight in Madrid.

Jez: What? You went to a bullfight? I'm surprised.

Tom: Really? _why do you_____?
                         1

Jez: _____Because_____ it's cruel, isn't it? Why would you
2

want to watch that?

Tom: Well, _____first of all_____, it's an important part of the
3

culture ... you know? _____ it's really popular.
4

Lots of tourists were there. It's _____good~~ also~~_____ good to
5

experience something different for a change ... I think.

B. Work in a group. Look at the activities in the box. Discuss which activities
you would like to try. Give reasons for your ideas.

white-water rafting

bungee jumping	shopping	white-water rafting
gardening	surfing	rock-climbing
other: _____		

A: *I'd like to try white-water rafting. That sounds amazing.*

B: *Really? Why do you say that? I think it sounds scary.*

A: *Well, first of all, I love water sports, and another reason is
that it looks very exciting.*

iQ ONLINE **C.** Go online for more practice asking for and giving reasons.

Unit Assignment Take part in a group discussion

UNIT OBJECTIVE ▶▶▶▶

In this assignment, you are going to take part in a group discussion about
the advantages and disadvantages of change. As you prepare for the group
discussion, think about the Unit Question, "Is change good or bad?" Use
information from Listening 1, Listening 2, the unit video, and your work in this
unit to support your discussion. Refer to the Self-Assessment checklist on page 74.

CONSIDER THE IDEAS

Work in a group. Think about the following important events that can occur
in people's lives. Each event represents a big change. Discuss the advantages
and disadvantages that each event might have. Use phrases from the
Speaking Skill box on page 71 to practice giving and asking for reasons.

changing your job	passing an exam
getting married	starting at a new school/college
studying abroad	

PREPARE AND SPEAK

A. **GATHER IDEAS** Think about the events you discussed with your group. Choose one of the events that you have experienced yourself. Then write answers to the questions.

Which event did you choose? _____

Did you experience the advantages and disadvantages you discussed with your group? What were they?

_____

_____

_____

_____

_____

What did you learn from this event?

_____

_____

_____

B. **ORGANIZE IDEAS** Complete the outline. Use ideas from your discussion and your notes from Activity A. Think about change in general as you answer the questions. Do not write exactly what you are going to say. Just write notes to help you organize your ideas.

What are the advantages of change?

_____

_____

_____

_____

What are the disadvantages of change?

_____

_____

_____

What can we learn from change?

_____

_____

_____

Tip for Success

When listening to your classmates, take notes of the main points each person makes. You can use these notes later when you want to ask questions.

C. SPEAK Discuss your ideas in a group. Do not read exactly what you wrote. Just use your notes. Use phrases from the Speaking Skill box on page 71 to give and ask for reasons. Decide who in your group has a view of change similar to your own. Refer to the Self-Assessment checklist below before you begin.

 Go online for your alternate Unit Assignment.

CHECK AND REFLECT

A. CHECK Think about the Unit Assignment as you complete the Self-Assessment checklist.

SELF-ASSESSMENT		
Yes	**No**	
☐	☐	I was able to speak easily about the topic.
☐	☐	My group understood me.
☐	☐	I used vocabulary from the unit.
☐	☐	I used tag questions.
☐	☐	I used intonation in tag questions.
☐	☐	I asked for reasons for someone's opinion and gave reasons for my own opinions.

B. REFLECT Go to the Online Discussion Board to discuss these questions.

1. What is something new you learned in this unit?

2. Look back at the Unit Question—Is change good or bad? Is your answer different now than when you started this unit? If yes, how is it different? Why?

TRACK YOUR SUCCESS

Circle the words and phrases you have learned in this unit.

Nouns
crisis 🔑   أزمة
position 🔑   موقف
research 🔑 AWL   بحث
wages 🔑   فلوس/راتب

Verbs
adapt 🔑 AWL   اقتنع
change 🔑   يغير
cope 🔑   كيف تتعامل
get 🔑   يعطي
handle 🔑
justify 🔑 AWL   كلل
struggle 🔑   مشكلة
suffer 🔑   يتألم
support (oneself) 🔑

Adjectives
curious 🔑   فضولي
exhausted   تعبان
fulfilled   سوي الشيء
informed   قال
permanent 🔑   إلا الأبد
steady 🔑
unemployed 🔑   غير موظف

Adverbs
Also, 🔑
considerably 🔑 AWL
Finally, 🔑 AWL
First, 🔑
firsthand
Second, 🔑

Phrases
Another reason/thing
  is …
Can you explain why …?
First of all,
That's why …
The reason … is (that) …
What are your reasons
  for saying that?
Why do you think/say
  that?

🔑 Oxford 3000™ words
AWL Academic Word List

Check (✓) the skills you learned. If you need more work on a skill, refer to the page(s) in parentheses.

NOTE TAKING ■	I can use a chart to take notes on advantages and disadvantages. (p. 55)
LISTENING ■	I can listen for time markers. (p. 60)
VOCABULARY ■	I can use word webs. (p. 66)
GRAMMAR ■	I can use tag questions. (p. 68)
PRONUNCIATION ■	I can use intonation in tag questions. (p. 70)
SPEAKING ■	I can ask for and give reasons. (p. 71)
UNIT OBJECTIVE ▶▶▶▶ ■	I can gather information and ideas to participate in a group discussion about change.

UNIT 4

Marketing

LISTENING ▶ identifying fact and opinion
VOCABULARY ▶ context clues to identify meaning
GRAMMAR ▶ modals expressing attitude
PRONUNCIATION ▶ intonation in questions
SPEAKING ▶ giving and supporting your opinions
NOTE TAKING ▶ using a mind map to note opinions

UNIT QUESTION

How can advertisers change our behavior?

A Discuss these questions with your classmates.

1. When you watch television, do you usually watch the commercials? What television ads can you think of right now?

2. How often do you click on Internet ads? Do you buy things on the Internet?

3. Look at the photos. What kinds of advertisements do you see?

B Listen to *The Q Classroom* online. Then answer these questions.

1. Marcus thinks that advertising makes a product seem more familiar to us, and as a result we are more likely to buy it. Do you agree? Did you ever buy something because you saw an ad?

2. Felix says that advertising helps companies become more famous, and people tend to trust famous companies more than companies they don't know. Do you agree? Which companies do you trust?

PIZZA THURSDAYS!
*Large Pizza
$3 off before 7 pm
*Small Pizza
2 for 1 before 7pm

iQ ONLINE **C** Go online to watch a video about innovative marketing. Then check your comprehension.

consensus *(n.)* an opinion that all members of a group agree with

open the floodgates *(phr.)* start something that will be difficult to stop

put up *(phr. v.)* installed

subliminally *(adv.)* affecting your mind even though you are not aware of it

VIDEO VOCABULARY

iQ ONLINE **D** Go to the Online Discussion Board to discuss the Unit Question with your classmates.

E Complete the questionnaire.

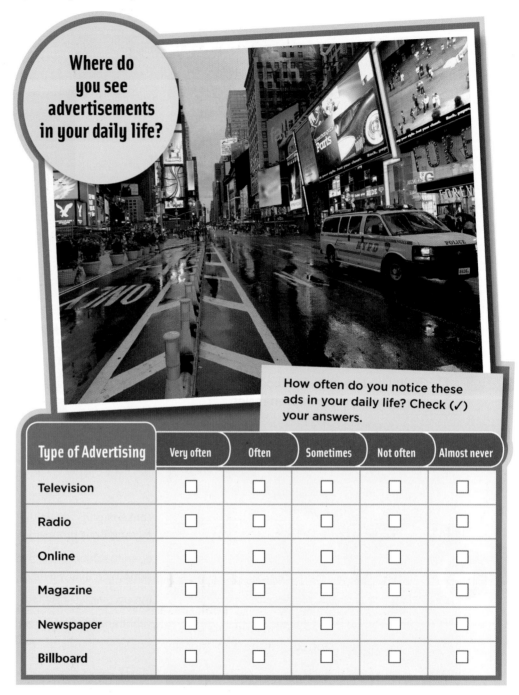

Where do you see advertisements in your daily life?

How often do you notice these ads in your daily life? Check (✓) your answers.

Type of Advertising	Very often	Often	Sometimes	Not often	Almost never
Television	☐	☐	☐	☐	☐
Radio	☐	☐	☐	☐	☐
Online	☐	☐	☐	☐	☐
Magazine	☐	☐	☐	☐	☐
Newspaper	☐	☐	☐	☐	☐
Billboard	☐	☐	☐	☐	☐

F Compare your answers with a partner. What are the advantages and disadvantages of each type of advertising? Which types do you pay most attention to?

LISTENING

LISTENING 1 | Advertising Techniques

UNIT OBJECTIVE ▶▶▶▶ You are going to listen to a group of students giving a presentation. As you listen to the presentation, gather information and ideas about how advertisers can change our behavior.

PREVIEW THE LISTENING

A class was given an assignment to research advertising on local radio. One group of students is presenting their ideas to the class, explaining various advertising techniques used in the ads they heard.

A. `PREVIEW` What kinds of products do you expect to hear advertised on the radio? Think of five products and write them down. Then share your ideas with the class.

B. `VOCABULARY` Read aloud these words from Listening 1. Check (✓) the ones you know. Use a dictionary to define any new or unknown words. Then discuss with a partner how the words will relate to the unit.

appeal *(n.)* 🔑	**logo** *(n.)*
brand *(n.)* 🔑	**memorable** *(adj.)*
campaign *(n.)* 🔑	**persuade** *(v.)* 🔑
claim *(v.)* 🔑	**relate to** *(phr.)* 🔑

🔑 Oxford 3000™ words

iQ `ONLINE` **C.** Go online to listen and practice your pronunciation.

WORK WITH THE LISTENING

🔊 **A.** `LISTEN AND TAKE NOTES` Look at the advertising techniques in the chart. Listen to the students give their presentation. Take notes on each advertising technique they mention.

Advertising technique	Notes
Emotional appeal	
Association of ideas	
Bandwagon	
Repetition	
Humor	

B. Use your notes to match each ad with a technique from the chart.

Name of ad

1. Dan's Diner _e_

2. Seattle Security ____

3. Robertson's Black ____

4. Perfect Pens ____

5. Arizona Market ____

Now match the descriptions in the box to the techniques in the chart. Compare your ideas with a partner. Then listen again and check your answers.

Technique	Description of technique
a. Emotional appeal	
b. Humor	
c. Bandwagon	g
d. Association of ideas	
e. Repetition	

f. links the product with positive ideas
g. claims the product is very popular
h. focuses on feelings and emotions
i. gives key information over and over again
j. makes people laugh

C. Read the statements. Write *T* (true) or *F* (false). Correct the false statements.

____ 1. There is no charge for a security assessment from Seattle Security.

____ 2. Seattle Security specializes in fitting high-quality alarms.

____ 3. Robertson's Black is a chocolate bar made in Switzerland.

____ 4. Arizona Market is a family event that takes place next Saturday.

____ 5. Arizona Market starts at noon.

____ 6. The special offer at Dan's Diner is available all week.

____ 7. There is no charge for teenagers at Dan's Diner.

____ 8. There are three varieties of Perfect Pens.

D. With a partner, decide which advertising technique to use with each of these products. Take notes of your reasons. Then make a group and explain your ideas.

1. A baby stroller	2. A fragrance for men	3. A cell phone

 E. Go online to listen to *Marketing Social Change* and check your comprehension.

F. **VOCABULARY** Use the new vocabulary from Listening 1. Read the sentences. Circle the answer that best matches the meaning of each word or phrase in bold.

Tip for Success

Keep a small notebook with you for new words and phrases. Check your notes when you get home.

1. I don't like negative advertising. I can't understand its **appeal**.
   a. attraction   b. title   c. product

2. This **brand** of toothpaste is the best one on the market.
   a. design   b. management   c. kind

3. The ad **campaign** was expensive, but it didn't produce great results.
   a. promotion   b. sample   c. poster

4. Many ads **claim** that their products have fantastic benefits, but don't give any proof.
   a. imagine   b. state   c. suppose

5. Everyone wore T-shirts showing the company's new **logo** of a jumping tiger.
   a. product   b. design   c. example

6. That company won the award for the most **memorable** ad of the year. People were still talking about it months afterwards.
   a. current   b. unforgettable   c. exciting

7. Advertisers use several techniques to **persuade** consumers to buy certain products.

    a. support   b. instruct   c. convince

8. Ads often try to **relate to** us on an emotional level.

    a. reply to   b. connect with   c. help

 G. Go online for more practice with the vocabulary.

SAY WHAT YOU THINK

Discuss the questions in a group.

1. Which radio ads in Listening 1 do you like most? Why?

2. Which advertising technique do you think is the most effective? Explain your reasons.

3. Think of an ad you have seen or heard recently. What product was it advertising? Which technique did it use? How effective do you think it was?

Listening Skill **Identifying fact and opinion**

When you listen, it is important to identify what is a **fact** and what is someone's **opinion**.

A fact is something that is always true and can be proved.

    Paris is the capital of France.
    Soccer matches last 90 minutes.

An opinion is something that cannot be proved. People might disagree about an opinion.

    Paris is the most beautiful city in the world.
    Soccer is a great game for young children.

 A. Listen to these statements from the radio ads you heard in Listening 1. Decide whether each statement is a fact or an opinion. Circle your answers.

1. fact / opinion

2. fact / opinion

3. fact / opinion

Tip for Success

The next time you listen to the radio, focus on the ads. Listen carefully, and try to identify what is fact and what is opinion.

B. Now listen to statements from another ad describing a personal computer. Decide whether each statement is a fact or an opinion. Circle your answers.

1. fact / opinion

2. fact / opinion

3. fact / opinion

4. fact / opinion

5. fact / opinion

6. fact / opinion

iQ ONLINE **C.** Go online for more practice identifying fact and opinion.

LISTENING 2 | Advertising Ethics and Standards

UNIT OBJECTIVE ▶▶▶ You are going to listen to an interview with Mary Engle, associate director for advertising practices at the U.S. Federal Trade Commission (FTC). As you listen to the interview, gather information and ideas about how advertisers can change our behavior.

PREVIEW THE LISTENING

The Federal Trade Commission is an independent agency of the U.S. government. It is responsible for keeping American business competition free and fair. Mary Engle directs the Division of Advertising Practices. The Division is responsible for regulating national advertising matters, including claims about food, OTC (over the counter) drugs, dietary supplements, and Internet services.

A. PREVIEW Mary Engle explains some of the ways in which advertising is controlled. In what ways do you think companies that break the advertising rules can be punished? Make a list of your ideas, and then compare with a partner.

B. **VOCABULARY** Read aloud these words from Listening 2. Check (✓) the ones you know. Use a dictionary to define any new or unknown words. Then discuss with a partner how the words will relate to the unit.

aimed at *(phr.)* 🔑	mislead *(v.)*
competitor *(n.)*	monitor *(v.)* 🔑
deliberately *(adv.)* 🔑	refund *(n.)*
evidence *(n.)* 🔑	regulations *(n.)* 🔑
injury *(n.)* 🔑	withdraw *(v.)* 🔑

🔑 Oxford 3000™ words

 C. Go online to listen and practice your pronunciation.

WORK WITH THE LISTENING

A. **LISTEN AND TAKE NOTES** Listen to the interview and take notes in the chart.

1. How the FTC finds ads that break the rules	
2. Examples of ways advertisers can be punished	

B. Read the statements. Write *T* (true) or *F* (false) according to what Mary Engle says. Correct the false statements.

_____ 1.   The FTC makes sure ads don't break the law.

_____

_____ 2.   Today there are fewer controls on advertising than in the past.

_____

_____ 3.   The FTC focuses mainly on health advertising.

_____

_____ 4.   Advertisers follow different regulations, depending on where the ad appears (for example, TV or radio).

_____

_____ 5. The FTC only checks ads on TV and radio.

_____

_____ 6. The FTC can take various steps to stop advertisers that break the rules.

_____

_____ 7. Monitoring advertising today is more difficult than in the past.

_____

_____ 8. The way companies advertise has not changed much over the years.

_____

C. **Read the sentences. Then listen again. Circle the answer that best completes each statement.**

1. The "truth-in-advertising" laws mean that advertisers shouldn't _____.
    a. advertise to children
    b. mislead the public
    c. make claims without providing evidence

2. As an example of untruthful advertising in the past, Engle mentions _____.
    a. weight loss products
    b. beauty products
    c. health food products

3. Engle says the main aim of the FTC is to make sure advertisers _____.
    a. don't overcharge people
    b. act responsibly
    c. don't criticize other companies

4. The FTC doesn't allow ads that might cause people to suffer physical or _____ harm.
    a. emotional
    b. personal
    c. financial

5. The FTC can only regulate _____ advertising.
    a. national
    b. state
    c. local

6. Engle gives an example of a fast food chain that broke the rules because _____.
    a. it claimed its food was healthy
    b. its food was too expensive
    c. its food made people ill

7. The FTC punished the fast food chain by _____.
    a. telling the company to withdraw the ad
    b. closing the company
    c. fining the company

8. Deliberately putting a funny video on the Internet that features a product is called _____.
    a. sub-viral marketing
    b. product placement
    c. Web promotion

Vocabulary Skill Review

In Unit 3, you learned that many words have more than one meaning. Use your dictionary to find any different meanings for each word, and make notes in your vocabulary notebook.

D. VOCABULARY Use the new vocabulary from Listening 2. Complete each sentence with the correct word from the list.

aimed at *(phr.)*	mislead *(v.)*
competitor *(n.)*	monitor *(v.)*
deliberately *(adv.)*	refund *(n.)*
evidence *(n.)*	regulations *(n.)*
injury *(n.)*	withdraw *(v.)*

1. The product didn't work, so the company had to give customers a(n) _____.

2. Advertisers may be given heavy fines if they _____ the public.

3. Ads for games are usually _____ children.

4. If a product causes _____ to customers, then the fines can be very large.

5. Sometimes companies have to _____ their products from the market because of faults.

6. It's important to _____ ads to check they are fair.

7. Unfortunately, our main _____ has a very good ad campaign at the moment.

8. The company claims that this ad resulted in more sales, but there isn't any _____ of that.

9. Companies that _____ give false information should pay a fine.

10. In the United States, each state decides its own advertising _____.

 E. Go online for more practice with the vocabulary.

SAY WHAT YOU THINK

A. Discuss the questions in a group.

1. Do you think product placement is a successful form of advertising? Explain your opinion. What product placement ads have you seen?

2. Which groups in society do you think are easy for advertisers to influence (children, teenagers, men, or women, for example)? Should advertising regulations be made stronger to protect these groups?

B. Think about the unit video, Listening 1, and Listening 2 as you discuss the questions.

1. What claims do advertisers make to influence people to buy their products (for example, "it's cheap," "it's healthy," etc.)? Make a list of examples from ads in this unit and from other ads you know.

Critical Thinking **Tip**

Question 2 of Activity B asks you to **evaluate** how truthful certain ad claims are. When you evaluate, you put your knowledge and opinions together.

2. Look at the claims you listed above. What products are likely to make these claims? Name one product for each claim and say whether that claim is usually truthful or not.

When you hear a word or phrase you don't know, it is sometimes possible to determine the meaning from the **context**. Try to identify the part of speech, and think about the words that surround it. Use this information to help you figure out what the word means.

☐ This magazine has a **circulation** of 100,000 a month.

Circulation is a noun. You can tell it refers to the number of copies of the magazine sold per month.

☐ We advertise a lot in video games because teenagers are our main **target**.

Target is a noun. You can tell it refers to the type of people that the ad is aimed at.

☐ **Infomercials** can mislead people into thinking they are watching a TV program.

Infomercial is the subject of the sentence and therefore a noun. You can see that it includes parts of two words you know: **info**rmation and com**mercial**. The context tells you that it refers to a type of TV program: an infomercial is a long commercial advertising a product.

A. Read the sentences. Underline the context clues that help you determine the meaning of each bold word. Compare your ideas with a partner.

1. That ad is so big and colorful. It's very **eye-catching**.

2. That radio station plays the same ads all day. It's **tedious** to hear them over and over.

3. Commercials in **prime time** are the most expensive because the largest number of people watch TV then.

4. We really need a more aggressive marketing strategy to **push** this product if we want it to sell more.

5. The ads for that new book are everywhere, but you shouldn't believe the **hype**. I read it, and it's terrible.

6. The slogan was so **catchy** I couldn't stop thinking about it for days.

B. Write each word from Activity A next to its correct definition. Compare your answers with your partner.

1. _____: to make something especially noticeable or attractive, so people will buy it

2. _____: interesting or attractive to look at

3. _____: the most popular time to watch TV

4. _____: advertising that makes something seem better than it is

5. _____: easy to remember

6. _____: boring and lasting a long time

iQ ONLINE **C.** Go online for more practice using context clues to identify meaning.

SPEAKING

 **UNIT OBJECTIVE** ▶▶▶▶ At the end of this unit, you will take part in a group discussion about how advertisers change our behavior. Make sure to give and support your opinions when you participate in the discussion.

Grammar | Modals expressing attitude

Modal verbs are special *auxiliary verbs* that help to express the attitude of the speaker. They are followed by the base form of the verb.

Prohibition:	They **must not** mislead anyone.
	They **can't** say anything false.
Strong obligation:	Ads **have to** be truthful.
	Ads **must** tell the truth.
Recommendation:	You **should** tell the FTC if an ad is misleading.
	You **shouldn't** believe everything you hear.
	There's another ad for that new restaurant. We **ought to** try it.
No obligation:	Advertisers **don't have to** send ads for approval.

Note: **Must/must not** are more common in writing than in conversation.

A. Listen to the conversation. Circle the modal verbs you hear. Then practice the conversation with a partner.

Yvonne: Oh, look at that ad. Those poor animals! How can they show them suffering like that? I think it's terrible!

Maureen: Really? I think it's quite effective. They're trying to get your attention, you know.

Yvonne: Well, they (<u>don't have to / can't</u>) do it that way! It's not necessary,
1
and it's upsetting.

Maureen: You (<u>must not / don't have to</u>) look at it if you don't want to.
2

Yvonne: That's not the point. That kind of advertising makes me really angry. I'm sure there's a law that says they (<u>don't have to / can't</u>) use animals
3
like that.

Maureen: Maybe you (<u>should / have to</u>) complain, then.
₄

Yvonne: Yes, I think I will. They (<u>shouldn't / don't have to</u>) be allowed to
₅

    do that!

B. Discuss these questions in a group. Use modals to express your attitude when possible.

1. What do you think about ads that might make people angry?

2. Are there any types of advertising that should not be allowed?

iQ ONLINE **C.** Go online for more practice using modals to express attitude.

D. Go online for the grammar expansion.

Pronunciation   **Part 1 Intonation in questions**

Intonation is different for **yes/no questions** than it is for **wh- questions** (questions that begin with *who, what, when, where, why, which,* or *how*). The intonation rises at the end of *yes/no* questions. It falls at the end of *wh-* questions.

Here are some examples from the interview with Mary Engle.

Yes/no questions

    Is there an advertising standards code?

    Are the rules the same in other countries?

Wh- questions

    How do you find ads that break the rules?

    What areas do you focus on in particular?

A. Listen to the questions. Does the intonation rise or fall at the end? Circle your answers.

1. Do you spend a lot of money on advertising?   rise / fall

2. What do you think of that ad?   rise / fall

3. Is that ad misleading?   rise / fall

4. Does it have a special offer?   rise / fall

5. Why is there so much hype these days?   rise / fall

B. Listen again. Repeat the questions. Use the same intonation that you hear.

| Pronunciation | *Part 2* Intonation in questions |

Statements as questions

Sometimes a statement is spoken with rising intonation to make it a question. This often happens if the speaker is surprised by what he has just heard.

Listen to how the intonation changes these statements into questions.

Statements

There are no federal regulations.

They're going to withdraw the product.

Questions

There are no federal regulations?

They're going to withdraw the product?

C. Listen to the sentences. Are they spoken as statements or questions? Circle the correct answer and complete each sentence with a period or question mark.

1. There are no federal regulations __?__   statement / (question)

2. The company is giving a refund to all its customers ____   statement / question

3. You're going to withdraw the product ____   statement / question

4. That ad is really annoying ____   statement / question

5. There used to be no controls ____   statement / question

6. The rules aren't the same in other countries ____   statement / question

7. Viral marketing is becoming more popular ____   statement / question

D. **Listen again. Then practice with a partner. Take turns saying different sentences from Activity C and deciding whether each sentence is a statement or a question.**

iQ ONLINE **E.** **Go online for more practice with intonation in questions.**

Speaking Skill   **Giving and supporting your opinions**

It is often useful to support your opinion by giving reasons and examples. Here are some phrases you can use when you want to give your opinion.

Giving opinions

> I (don't) think (that)
> In my opinion/view,
> If you ask me,
> As far as I'm concerned,

Here are some phrases you can use to support your opinion.

Supporting opinions

> because/as
> For example,
> For instance,
> To give you an example,
>
> **In my opinion**, there's too much advertising on TV these days. **To give you an example**, a program I watched last night had ads almost every ten minutes! **If you ask me**, they shouldn't show ads in the middle of programs on TV.

 | Listening and Speaking   **93**

A. Listen to this conversation about an ad. Complete the conversation with the phrases that you hear. Then practice the conversation with a partner.

Hugo: Hey. Look at this ad. It's got six famous people in it!

Peter: So what? _____ 1 , they should spend less on these expensive ads and lower the price of their clothes.

Hugo: Hmm. But I like seeing famous people in ads _____ 2 it makes it kind of cool.

Peter: _____ 3 , there are better ways to advertise things. _____ 4 , they could have some facts and statistics or something. You know, some information …

Hugo: But it's an ad, right? _____ 5 , an ad should get people's attention, and using famous people does that.

Peter: Well, I guess it's eye-catching, but I'm not sure how effective it is.

B. Work with a partner. What do you think of ads that feature famous people? Are they effective? Discuss these questions. Use phrases from the Speaking Skill box to give and support your opinions.

iQ ONLINE **C.** Go online for more practice giving and supporting your opinions.

Note-taking Skill Using a mind map to note opinions

When discussing a topic, it can be useful to use a mind map. This is especially beneficial if you need to take notes on several different opinions. Using a mind map allows you to organize opinions and link supporting details to each opinion in a way that is easy to refer to later.

To make a mind map, first write the topic in the center and draw a circle around it. Then note all the different opinions by drawing a separate line for each opinion outward from the circle. You can add any supporting facts and details next to or below each opinion, as shown in the mind map below.

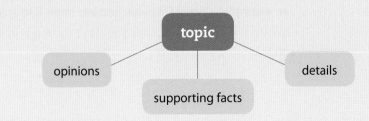

A. Study this mind map of a discussion on celebrity advertising. Notice how the opinions are noted separately along with their supporting ideas.

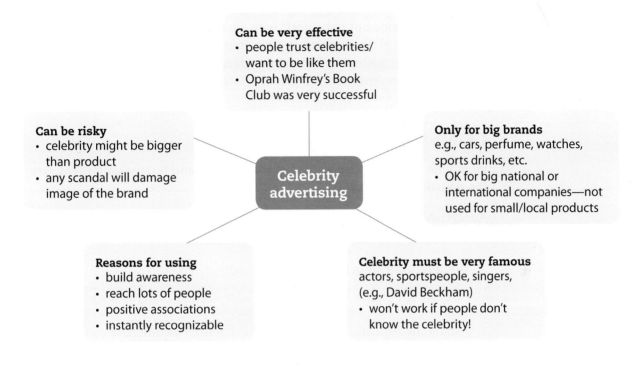

Can be very effective
- people trust celebrities/ want to be like them
- Oprah Winfrey's Book Club was very successful

Can be risky
- celebrity might be bigger than product
- any scandal will damage image of the brand

Celebrity advertising

Only for big brands
e.g., cars, perfume, watches, sports drinks, etc.
- OK for big national or international companies—not used for small/local products

Reasons for using
- build awareness
- reach lots of people
- positive associations
- instantly recognizable

Celebrity must be very famous
actors, sportspeople, singers, (e.g., David Beckham)
- won't work if people don't know the celebrity!

B. Discuss the topic of celebrity advertising using the mind map in Activity A to help you. Add any additional opinions and supporting details.

C. Fill in the mind map below to prepare for a discussion on what makes an advertisement effective. Write your opinions and supporting details in the empty circles. Then discuss your opinions with a partner.

What makes an advertisement effective?

 D. Go online for more practice using a mind map to note opinions.

In this assignment, you are going to discuss the Unit Question, "How can advertisers change our behavior?" with a partner. Then you will summarize your discussion in a group and explain your own opinion. Use information from Listening 1, Listening 2, the unit video, and your work in this unit to support your presentation. Refer to the Self-Assessment checklist on page 98.

CONSIDER THE IDEAS

Work with a partner. Choose one of these topics and discuss your ideas. Use the questions to help you.

Advertising and children

1. What kinds of products are advertised to children?

2. What types of advertising are often used?

3. How are ads aimed at children different from ads aimed at adults?

4. Should the regulations for ads aimed at children be different?

5. Should advertising to children be banned?

Health ads

1. What kinds of health products are advertised?

2. What kind of person is influenced by health ads?

3. Are you influenced by health ads?

4. Should the regulations for health ads be stricter than they are for other ads?

5. Should the advertising of unhealthy products be banned?

Status

1. What kinds of products are advertised as "high class"?

2. Who do you think is the target for these kinds of status ads?

3. Are the claims made by status ads misleading?

4. Why are so many people influenced by this type of advertising?

5. Are you influenced by this type of advertising?

PREPARE AND SPEAK

A. GATHER IDEAS Write the topic you chose in the Consider the Ideas activity in the center of the mind map. Then note your answers to each question (1–5) in the space provided. If necessary, add more lines to help you note any additional ideas or opinions.

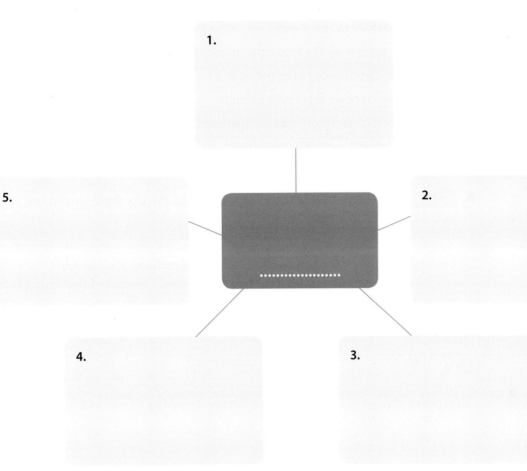

B. ORGANIZE IDEAS Support your opinions by adding facts and details. Make notes next to or below each opinion to explain your reasons.

C. SPEAK Have a group discussion about how advertisers can influence our behavior. Refer to the Self-Assessment checklist on page 98 before you begin.

1. Take turns presenting your ideas from Activity B.

2. You can refer to your notes, but do not read exactly what you wrote.

3. Give each student a turn as group leader.

iQ ONLINE **Go online for your alternate Unit Assignment.**

CHECK AND REFLECT

A. `CHECK` **Think about the Unit Assignment as you complete the Self-Assessment checklist.**

Yes	No	SELF-ASSESSMENT
☐	☐	I was able to speak easily about the topic.
☐	☐	My partner and group understood me.
☐	☐	I used vocabulary from the unit.
☐	☐	I used modals expressing attitude.
☐	☐	I used correct intonation in questions.
☐	☐	I gave and supported my opinion.

B. `REFLECT` **Go to the Online Discussion Board to discuss these questions.**

1. What is something new you learned in this unit?

2. Look back at the Unit Question — How can advertisers change our behavior? Is your answer different now than when you started this unit? If yes, how is it different? Why?

TRACK YOUR SUCCESS

Circle the words and phrases you have learned in this unit.

Nouns
appeal 🔑
brand 🔑
campaign 🔑
circulation
competitor
evidence 🔑 AWL
hype
infomercial
injury 🔑 AWL
logo
refund
regulations 🔑 AWL
slogan
target 🔑 AWL

Verbs
claim 🔑
mislead
monitor 🔑 AWL
persuade 🔑
push 🔑
withdraw 🔑

Adjectives
catchy
eye-catching
memorable
tedious

Adverbs
deliberately 🔑

Phrases
aimed at 🔑
As far as I'm concerned,
because/as
For example,
For instance,
I (don't) think (that)
If you ask me,
In my opinion,
In my view,
prime time
relate to 🔑
To give you an example,

🔑 Oxford 3000™ words
AWL Academic Word List

Check (✓) the skills you learned. If you need more work on a skill, refer to the page(s) in parentheses.

LISTENING ☐	I can identify fact and opinion. (p. 82)
VOCABULARY ☐	I can identify meaning from context. (p. 88)
GRAMMAR ☐	I can use modals to express attitude. (p. 90)
PRONUNCIATION ☐	I can use correct intonation in questions. (pp. 91–92)
SPEAKING ☐	I can give and support my opinions. (p. 93)
NOTE TAKING ☐	I can use a mind map to note opinions. (p. 94)
UNIT OBJECTIVE ▶▶▶▶ ☐	I can gather information and ideas to state and support my opinions in a group discussion on advertising.

UNIT 5

NOTE TAKING	▶	separating risks and outcomes using a chart
LISTENING	▶	identifying amounts; cardinal and ordinal numbers
VOCABULARY	▶	word families
GRAMMAR	▶	past perfect
PRONUNCIATION	▶	contraction of *had*
SPEAKING	▶	giving a short presentation

Behavioral Science

Q UNIT QUESTION

What risks are good to take?

A Discuss these questions with your classmates.

1. What are some risks that people take? Why do they take them?

2. What kinds of risks are OK to take? What kinds are not? Why?

3. Look at the photo. What kind of a risk is this man taking? Would you ever take this kind of risk? Why or why not?

B Listen to *The Q Classroom* online. Then answer these questions.

1. What types of risks do the students mention?

2. Why is it good to take social risks? What are the risks of changing jobs?

iQ ONLINE **C** Go to the Online Discussion Board to discuss the Unit Question with your classmates.

UNIT ▶▶▶▶ Listen to a talk and a report and gather information
OBJECTIVE   and ideas to give a short presentation on a risk you
                have taken.

D Look at the questionnaire. Check (✓) your answers. Then read the answers below to find out if you are a risk taker.

Are you a risk taker?

Have you ever:	Yes, I have.	No, but I might.	No, I never will.
1 moved to a new country?	☐	☐	☐
2 gone on vacation without a place to stay?	☐	☐	☐
3 bought something you couldn't afford?	☐	☐	☐
4 done something others might think crazy?	☐	☐	☐
5 slept outside without a tent?	☐	☐	☐
6 stayed up late the night before an exam?	☐	☐	☐
7 made a promise that might be difficult to keep?	☐	☐	☐
8 ridden on the back of a motorcycle?	☐	☐	☐

Rate your answers

If you answered mostly yes: You like to take many different kinds of risks. You may get a thrill by taking risks. Life is fast and exciting. Sometimes, the risk will be worth it, but you could get into trouble.

If you answered mostly no: You play it safe. You are uncomfortable with risks. Your idea of a good time is staying home and reading a book. The good thing is that you will avoid trouble. On the other hand, you may not be as successful as some risk takers.

If your answers were mostly in the middle column or included some of each: You are middle-of-the-road. You are willing to take some risks, but not too many. You're careful, but willing to put yourself in uncomfortable situations if it's worth it.

E Discuss the answers in a group. Do you agree with the description of you? Why or why not? Give examples.

When people take risks, they do it because they want one or more outcomes. An outcome is a result, or an effect, of taking a certain action. When listening to a speaker talking about risks and outcomes, you can list the risks and outcomes for an action separately in a chart.

Action: Moving to a new city

Risks	Desired Outcomes
• far away from friends/family	• find a better job in field
• have to quit job	• take classes at the university
• no apartment	• meet new people

Signposts to listen for:

One possible risk is . . .   *I hope to . . .*
This is risky because . . .   *She wants to . . .*
One danger of this is . . .   *We take the risk in order to . . .*
You risk . . .   *. . . far outweighs any risk.*
It threatens . . .

A. **Read this excerpt from a presentation about a new hobby. Then answer the questions on page 104.**

For the past several years, I have played soccer every Thursday night on a club team. This year, I decided to try something different. I wanted to learn how to kayak but the class was on Thursday nights. I was nervous. Signing up for the kayaking class was a little risky because I would lose my spot on the soccer team. Also, I know how to play soccer, and I might be bad at kayaking. But I wanted to try something new. I was a little bored with soccer. Kayaking is also great exercise, and it is a new skill. I use different muscles. Also, I am meeting new people. You can kayak with other people, or you can kayak by yourself, so it's more flexible.

Kayaking

1. What action does the speaker talk about? _____

2. What were some risks?

   _____

   _____

3. What outcomes did the speaker hope for?

   _____

   _____

B. With a partner, summarize the speaker's points on the chart below.

Action:	
Risks	**Outcome**

iQ ONLINE **C.** Go online for more practice separating risks and outcomes with a chart.

LISTENING 1 | Write Your Own Success Story

You are going to listen to a book reviewer talk about different risks writers take to get published. As you listen to the talk, gather information and ideas about what risks are good to take.

PREVIEW THE LISTENING

A. PREVIEW What are two risks a writer might take in order to get his or her book published?

B. VOCABULARY Read aloud these words and phrases from Listening 1. Check (✓) the ones you know. Use a dictionary to define any new or unknown words. Then discuss with a partner how the words will relate to the unit.

audience (n.) 🔑	**income** (n.) 🔑
embarrass (v.) 🔑	**model** (n.) 🔑
expose (v.) 🔑	**promote** (v.) 🔑
financial (adj.) 🔑	**publish** (v.) 🔑
funds (n.) 🔑	**threaten** (v.) 🔑

🔑 Oxford 3000™ words

C. Go online to listen and practice your pronunciation.

WORK WITH THE LISTENING

A. LISTEN AND TAKE NOTES Listen to the talk about publishing. Before you listen, look at the chart below. As you listen, add information to the chart.

Writer	Action	Outcome
John Grisham		
Christopher Paolini and parents		
Brunonia Barry		
Amanda Hocking		

B. Work with a partner. Complete the chart with information from activity A.

Self-publishing and marketing	
Risks	**Outcome**

C. Read the statements. Write *T* (true) or *F* (false). Write supporting information from the listening. Then correct each false statement to make it true.

	Supporting information in the listening
__T__ **1.** For a long time, publishing your own book was a risk to your reputation.	It was embarrassing.
____ **2.** Publishers typically pay authors a large advance and also pay to promote the book.	
____ **3.** It's not hard to promote your own book.	
____ **4.** Even when a person publishes his or her own book, a major publisher may decide to buy it later.	
____ **5.** Because e-books are inexpensive to produce, they can be made available to more people.	

D. Listen again. Write the missing details in the chart.

Writer	Type of book	First publisher	What the writer did (strategies)
John Grisham		very small publishing company	
	adventure novel		
		their own software company	
Amanda Hocking			

E. Based on the information in the listening, complete each sentence with the best phrase.

1. Writers who publish their own books today get ___ those in the past.
   a. less respect than
   b. the same amount of respect as
   c. more respect than

2. For successful self-publishers, publication of the book is probably ___.
   a. the final step in a long process
   b. the beginning of a new stage of the process
   c. fairly easy

3. The speaker probably thinks self-publishing is ___.
   a. a bad idea
   b. an excellent idea
   c. an idea writers should think about

F. Read the situations below. All three of these people have written books, but can't find a publisher. Which strategies used by other writers do you think they should try? Discuss with a partner. Explain your reasons.

1. Marisa Jackson just graduated from college. She has written three young adult novels set in a strange new world. She uses social media a lot.

2. Howard Hart is a middle-aged lawyer. His work keeps him very busy. He has a lot of money in savings. He wrote an exciting courtroom drama.

3. Elena Marx is a single parent with two children in college. She works as an accountant and part-time in a bookstore. She has written and illustrated three children's books.

G. VOCABULARY Use the new vocabulary from Listening 1. Read the paragraph. Then fill in the blanks with the correct words from the list.

| audience *(n.)* | expose *(v.)* | funds *(n.)* | model *(n.)* | publish *(v.)* |
| embarrass *(v.)* | financial *(adj.)* | income *(n.)* | promote *(v.)* | threaten *(v.)* |

Learning about Money the Hard Way

When I went to college, I didn't know anything about

_____ matters. I didn't have very much money.
             1

I wasn't working, so I didn't have a regular _____.
                                                              2

I started to buy things online or that I saw on TV. If an ad came on to

_____ a new product, I just had to have it. That way I could
             3

buy whatever I wanted without paying right away. Soon, I had a $25,000

credit card bill. When my parents found the bill, they were very upset.

They offered to give me the _____ I needed to pay it. They
                                              4

didn't want to _____ me, but told me I needed to be more
                       5

responsible. I finally repaid them, but it took a long time. Now I work for

a bank and give talks to college students about managing their money. I

try to _____ the problems they can have if they owe a lot of
              6

money when they are in school. I explain that what I did was not a good

_____ to follow. The students in the _____
             7   8

are always interested in the topic. They usually don't know that owing

so much money can _____ their future happiness.
                            9

We are going to _____ a book soon about money and
                         10

college students.

iQ ONLINE **H.** Go online for more practice with the vocabulary.

SAY WHAT YOU THINK

Discuss the questions in a group.

1. Why do you think these writers took the risks they did?

2. Do you have any dreams or goals that might require you to take risks? What are they? What are some of the risks you might have to take to achieve them?

3. What careers do you think involve a lot of risk? Why?

Listening Skill | **Part 1 Identifying amounts; cardinal and ordinal numbers**

Identifying amounts

When listening to amounts of money, first listen for the amounts (*fifty, one hundred, two thousand, million, billion*). Then listen for the units or currency (*dollars, euros, pounds*). It is important to remember that the way you say and hear amounts of money is different from the way you write them or see them when reading. For example, you will read and write *$300*, but you will hear *three hundred dollars*.

 Listen to these examples.

$500	$200,000
£1,000	£5,000,000
€10,000	€12,000,000,000

Listen to this excerpt from Listening 1 and pay attention to the amounts you hear. Notice that the $, £, or € sign is always written to show amounts of money, but it is not always spoken, especially after the first reference.

> They risked their savings, spending $50,000 on the publication and publicity.
> She sold the rights for $2 million.

Using amounts as adjectives

> It was a **fifty-dollar** shirt.
> The **three-hundred-pound** football player needed a larger uniform.
> The **four-hundred-seat** stadium was too small for the crowd.
> It's a **fifteen-minute** bus ride to my office.

When you write an amount as an adjective before a noun, use hyphens between each word of the adjective. Notice that it is not in the plural.

> ✓ A five-hundred-dollar TV.
> ✗ A five-hundred-dollars TV.

A. Listen to the sentences. Complete the sentences with the amounts you hear. Do not write the dollar sign ($). Write out the amounts in words. If the amount is an adjective, use hyphens.

1. Christopher Paolini sold the rights to his novels for

   _____.

2. The cheapest tickets are _____.

3. The _____ bag of sugar is _____.

4. The _____ stadium was too small for the crowd.

5. That store sells _____ shoes.

6. We took a _____ survey online.

7. My suitcase weighs over _____.

8. Maria found a _____ bill on the sidewalk.

B. Work with a partner. Take turns asking and answering questions about the sentences in Activity A.

A: How much did Paolini sell his book rights for?
B: He sold them for five hundred thousand dollars.

Listening Skill	**Part 2 Identifying amounts; cardinal and ordinal numbers**

Identifying cardinal and ordinal numbers

Some **ordinal** numbers sound very different from **cardinal** numbers (*first/one, second/two, third/three*). Most sound very similar except they end in a *–th* sound (*sixteen/sixteenth, thirty/thirtieth*).

Listen to these cardinal and ordinal numbers. Pay attention to the *–th* sound at the end of most ordinal numbers.

cardinal	ordinal	cardinal	ordinal
one	first	seven	seventh
two	second	twenty	twentieth
three	third	thirty-four	thirty-fourth
five	fifth	forty-six	forty-sixth

C. Listen to the sentences. Check (✓) the sentence you hear.

1. ☐ The seven tests can be taken this week.
   ☐ The seventh test can be taken this week.

2. ☐ The nine students left an hour ago.
   ☐ The ninth student left an hour ago.

3. ☐ I ate the fifteen cookies.
   ☐ I ate the fifteenth cookie.

4. ☐ Did you receive the six emails I sent you?
   ☐ Did you receive the sixth email I sent you?

5. ☐ Push the four buttons.
   ☐ Push the fourth button.

D. Listen again. Repeat the sentences. Then take turns saying and identifying the sentences from Activity C with a partner.

iQ ONLINE

E. Go online for more practice identifying amounts and cardinal and ordinal numbers.

LISTENING 2 | Science on the Edge

UNIT OBJECTIVE ▶▶▶▶ You are going to listen to a report on scientists with risky jobs. As you listen to the report, gather information and ideas about what risks are good to take.

PREVIEW THE LISTENING

A. PREVIEW Which fields of science do you think are risky?

☐ drug research   ☐ studying volcanoes

☐ laboratory research   ☐ underwater exploration

☐ meteorology (weather)   ☐ your idea: _____

B. VOCABULARY Read aloud these words and phrases from Listening 2. Check (✓) the ones you know. Use a dictionary to define any new or unknown words. Then discuss with a partner how the words will relate to the unit.

discover (v.) 🔑	investigate (v.) 🔑	mystery (n.) 🔑	prove (v.) 🔑	retire (v.) 🔑
invention (n.) 🔑	locate (v.) 🔑	previous (adj.) 🔑	reputation (n.) 🔑	solve (v.) 🔑

🔑 Oxford 3000™ words

C. Go online to listen and practice your pronunciation.

WORK WITH THE LISTENING

A. **LISTEN AND TAKE NOTES** Listen to the report. Take notes in the chart as you listen.

	Risks taken	Outcomes
Paul Flaherty		
Tina Neal		

B. Work with a partner. Answer the questions with information from the chart.

1. What risks do they both take?

2. What outcomes do both hope for?

C. Read the statements. Write *T* (true) or *F* (false). Then correct each false statement to make it true.

____ 1. Flaherty and Nepal work in the same scientific field.

_____

____ 2. Weather is one of the biggest risks they face.

_____

____ 3. Both scientists gather information to help predict natural disasters.

_____

____ 4. Unfortunately, there isn't much they can do to control or lower their risks.

_____

D. Listen again. Who is the detail about? Write *F* (Flaherty), *N* (Neal), or *B* (both) on the line.

____ 1. is a pilot

____ 2. flies a lot as part of the job

____ 3. makes maps of safe areas

____ 4. provided information on Hurricane Katrina

____ 5. lives in Alaska

____ 6. uses data to protect people

____ 7. works for National Oceanic and Atmospheric Administration

____ 8. works for the U.S. Geological Survey

E. Complete the Venn diagram with information about the two scientists.

Paul Flaherty   Both   Tina Neal

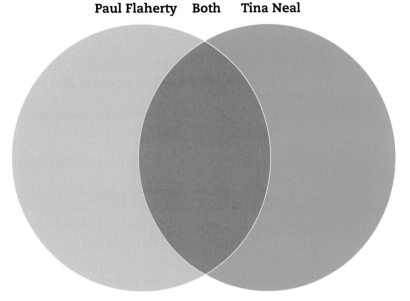

 F. Go online to listen to *The Blind Traveler* and check your comprehension.

Vocabulary Skill Review

In Unit 4, you learned how to use context clues to identify meaning. In Activity G, underline the clues in the sentences that help you identify the meaning of the words in bold.

G. **VOCABULARY** Use the new vocabulary from Listening 2. Read the sentences. Then write each bold word next to the correct definition.

1. Marie Curie was the first person to **discover** the elements polonium and radium.

2. My uncle's **invention** is a new machine that makes coffee and a doughnut at the same time.

3. For your next paper, I want you to **investigate** a topic that is interesting to you.

4. The police were unable to **locate** the stolen artifact.

5. Until recently, the nature of the planet Mars has been a **mystery**.

6. On my **previous** trip to Italy, I went to Venice, but I'm not going there this time.

7. Columbus was able to **prove** the earth was round.

8. That university has a very good **reputation**.

9. Dr. Arnesen enjoys his job so much, he says he never wants to **retire**.

10. Some of life's problems are too difficult for people to **solve** on their own.

a. _____ *(v.)* to find the exact position of someone or something

b. _____ *(v.)* to find a way of dealing with a problem or situation

c. _____ *(adj.)* coming or happening before or earlier

d. _____ *(v.)* to try to find out all the facts about something

e. _____ *(n.)* something that is made for the first time

f. _____ *(v.)* to stop working, usually because you have reached a certain age

g. _____ *(n.)* the opinion that people in general have about someone or something

h. _____ *(v.)* to use facts or evidence to show something is true

i. _____ *(n.)* a thing that you cannot understand or explain

j. _____ *(v.)* to find or learn something that no one knew or had found before

 H. Go online for more practice with the vocabulary.

SAY WHAT YOU THINK

A. Discuss the questions in a group.

1. Why do you think Flaherty and Neal are willing to take risks? Do you think they are different from most people? If so, how?

2. What other weather problems or natural disasters do we need to learn more about? What risks are involved in investigating them?

B. Before you watch the video, discuss the questions in a group.

1. What kinds of risks do scientists take today?

2. Why are people willing to try new and perhaps risky technologies?

 C. Go online to watch a video about a scientist collecting a sample from the Mount Nyiragongo volcano in the Democratic Republic of the Congo. Then check your comprehension.

> **deflect** *(v.)* to prevent something from being directed toward you
>
> **lava** *(n.)* hot liquid rock that comes out of a volcano
>
> **outrun** *(v.)* to run faster than
>
> **retreat** *(v.)* to move away or back
>
> **solidify** *(v.)* to become solid

VIDEO VOCABULARY

D. Think about the unit video, Listening 1, and Listening 2 as you discuss the questions.

1. Why do people take risks in their careers? Is this a good thing? Why or why not?

2. Do you think people are more likely to take risks for professional reasons or in their personal life? Explain.

Vocabulary Skill | Word families

One way to increase your vocabulary is to understand **word families**. Word families consist of words that come from the same root and are related in form. They usually include several different parts of speech. For example, a noun may have an adjective and a verb form. The ending of the word often indicates the part of speech.

> **in·vent** /ɪnˈvɛnt/ *verb* [T] **1** to think of or make something for the first time: *Who invented the sewing machine?* ◆ *When was the camera invented?* **2** to say or describe something that is not true: *I realized that he had invented the whole story.* ▶ **in·ven·tor** /ɪnˈvɛntər/ *noun* [C]
>
> **in·ven·tion** /ɪnˈvɛnʃn/ *noun* **1** [C] a thing that has been made or designed by someone for the first time: *The microwave oven is a very useful invention.* **2** [U] the action or process of making or designing something for the first time: *Books had to be written by hand before the invention of printing.* **3** [C, U] telling a story or giving an excuse that is not true: *This story is apparently a complete invention.*
>
> **in·ven·tive** /ɪnˈvɛntɪv/ *adj.* having new and interesting ideas ▶ **in·ven·tive·ness** *noun* [U]

When you look up new words in the dictionary, look at the other words in the same word family. By doing this, you can add several new words to your vocabulary.

Another benefit of understanding word families is that when you see new words that look similar to words you already know, you can use your knowledge to figure out their meaning.

All dictionary entries are from the *Oxford American Dictionary for learners of English*
© Oxford University Press 2011.

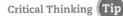

Critical Thinking **Tip**

The chart in Activity
A **categorizes** words
by their part of
speech. **Categorizing**
is placing things
into different
groups. It can help
you see similarities
within groups
and differences
between groups.

A. Work with a partner. Complete the word family chart with any forms of the words you know. Use a dictionary to check your answers.

Verb	Noun	Adjective	Adverb
invent	inventor	inventive	inventively
		creative	
discover			
embarrass			
		financial	
locate			
prove		proven	
solve			

B. Complete each sentence with an appropriate word from Activity A. You may need to change the form.

1. Children are often _____ in the ways they play.

2. I can't _____ this math problem.

3. The scientist made an important new _____.

4. Independent TV producers _____ their programs in different ways: from credit cards to private investors to personal savings.

5. The _____ to the problem is at the back of the book.

6. Having too much credit card debt can lead to _____ disaster.

7. Scientists have never found real _____ that aliens exist.

8. We decided not to buy the house because of its _____. It was too close to the freeway.

9. I can't _____ he took my money, but I think he did.

10. I spilled coffee all over the table and myself at the fancy restaurant last night—it was so _____!

iQ ONLINE **C.** Go online for more practice with word families.

SPEAKING

UNIT OBJECTIVE ▶▶▶▶ At the end of this unit, you will give a short presentation on a risk you have taken. Be sure to clearly explain your reasons for taking that risk.

Grammar | Past perfect

Use the **past perfect** to show the relationship between two events or actions that happened in the past. Use the past perfect to describe the first event or action that happened. Use the **simple past** to describe the second event or action.

Past perfect *(1st event)*	Simple past *(2nd event)*
I **had driven** for five hours.	I **went** straight to bed without dinner.

Past perfect *(1st event)*	Simple past *(2nd event)*
The match **had** already **started**.	We **arrived** late.

Use the past perfect with past time clauses that begin with *when, before, by the time,* and *until.*

Past perfect *(1st event)*	Simple past *(2nd event)*
He **had been** at work for hours	<u>when</u> we **called** him.
Paul **had driven** for an hour	<u>before</u> he **noticed** he had a flat tire.
They **had** already **eaten** dinner	<u>by the time</u> I **got** home.
I **hadn't heard** anything about it	<u>until</u> I **read** the paper this morning.

Note: The past perfect is often used with the adverbs *already, yet, never, ever,* and *just.*

A. Read the pairs of sentences. Write 1 next to the sentence that happened first. Write 2 next to the sentence that happened second. Then write one sentence. Use the past time clause in parentheses.

1. The scientist retired. __1__
   He began research on a new area of interest. __2__

   (before) <u>The scientist had retired before he began research on a new area of interest.</u>

2. I didn't hear about Brunonia Barry. ____
   I read the article. ____

   (until) _____

3. It started to rain. ____
   We finished hiking. ____

   (before) _____

4. Mari picked up the phone. ____
   It stopped ringing. ____

   (by the time) _____

5. My sister told me. ____
   I didn't realize my sweater was on backwards. ____

   (until) _____

6. Nawaf left his house. ____
   His mother called. ____

   (when) _____

7. I drank the cup of coffee. ____
   I realized it wasn't mine. ____

   (before) _____

8. We arrived at the airport. ____
   Our plane departed. ____

   (by the time) _____

B. Complete the sentences with information that is true for you. Then take turns reading your sentences with a partner.

1. I _____ when I got home yesterday.

2. I _____ until I started taking this class.

3. I _____ by the time I graduated from high school.

4. I _____ by the year 2000.

5. I _____ before I _____ .

iQ ONLINE

C. Go online for more practice using the past perfect.

D. Go online for the grammar expansion.

The contraction *'d* is frequently used instead of *had* in affirmative statements with the past perfect. Noticing *had* and the contraction *'d* can help you better understand the order of past events.

Listen to these examples. The speaker joins *'d* to words that follow beginning with vowel sounds and certain consonant sounds (*l, r*). Notice that *'d* is not stressed.

> I**'d** already finished the test when the teacher collected our papers.
> He**'d** eaten at that restaurant before.
> We**'d** often talked about getting married.
> You**'d** left when we got there.
> She**'d** written her email before she received mine.

Do not use a contraction with questions. Notice that *had* is not stressed in these questions.

> **Had** you heard from him by the time you left?
> **Had** everyone finished the test by 2:00?

The contraction with negatives is *hadn't*.

> I **hadn't** finished my phone call by the time the train arrived.
> They **hadn't** gone to the mall before they ate dinner.

A. Listen to the sentences. Check (✓) the sentence you hear.

1. ☐ He worked at a bookstore.
   ☐ He'd worked at a bookstore.

2. ☐ We left when it started raining.
   ☐ We'd left when it started raining.

3. ☐ They answered the questions.
   ☐ They'd answered the questions.

4. ☐ I've eaten my lunch.
   ☐ I'd eaten my lunch.

5. ☐ You've already taken the test.
   ☐ You'd already taken the test.

6. ☐ She didn't work there.

☐ She hadn't worked there.

7. ☐ It hasn't started to rain.

☐ It hadn't started to rain.

8. ☐ Has he found it?

☐ Had he found it?

9. ☐ Have you called Alex?

☐ Had you called Alex?

B. Listen again. Repeat the sentences. Then take turns saying and identifying the sentences from Activity A with a partner.

iQ ONLINE **C.** Go online for more practice with the contraction of *had*.

Speaking Skill | **Giving a short presentation**

When you give a short presentation in class or at work, start by introducing your topic clearly.

Here are some phrases you can use to introduce your topic.

> I want to talk about …
> My topic is …
> This presentation is on …
> I'm going to talk about …

During your presentation, it is important to use words and phrases that help your audience understand the order of events and the reasons for them.

Here are some words and phrases you can use to help your audience follow and understand your presentation.

Order of events	Purpose/reason
First,	so …
Second,	so that …
After that,	in order to …
Then,	The reason I took this risk was …
Before	
By the time	

A. Listen to this presentation. Complete the sentences with the words and phrases you hear.

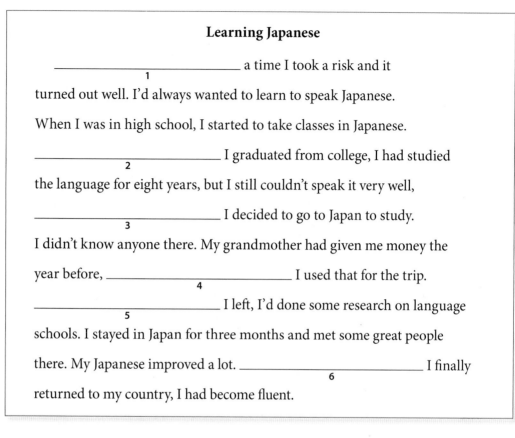

Learning Japanese

_____ a time I took a risk and it
            1
turned out well. I'd always wanted to learn to speak Japanese.

When I was in high school, I started to take classes in Japanese.

_____ I graduated from college, I had studied
            2
the language for eight years, but I still couldn't speak it very well,

_____ I decided to go to Japan to study.
            3
I didn't know anyone there. My grandmother had given me money the

year before, _____ I used that for the trip.
                        4
_____ I left, I'd done some research on language
            5
schools. I stayed in Japan for three months and met some great people

there. My Japanese improved a lot. _____ I finally
                                              6
returned to my country, I had become fluent.

Tip for Success

When listening, make sure you maintain eye contact. This encourages the speaker and shows that you are interested.

B. Check (✓) the risks you would take to learn English. Add some of your own ideas.

☐ join a club or sports team where people speak English
☐ take classes in other subjects with native English speakers
☐ move to a new city or country
☐ meet and talk to native speakers
☐ travel in English-speaking countries
☐ (your idea) _____
☐ (your idea) _____

C. Work with a partner. Take turns talking about the risks you checked in Activity B. Use words and phrases from the Speaking Skill box on page 120.

iQ ONLINE **D.** Go online for more practice with giving a short presentation.

UNIT OBJECTIVE ▶▶▶▶ In this assignment, you are going to give a one-minute presentation on a risk you have taken. As you prepare your presentation, think about the Unit Question, "What risks are good to take?" Use information from Listening 1, Listening 2, the unit video, and your work in this unit to support your presentation. Refer to the Self-Assessment checklist on page 124 .

CONSIDER THE IDEAS

🔊 Listen to one man talk about a risk he took and the reasons why he took it. Take notes as you listen. Then discuss the questions with a partner.

The Pantheon in Rome

A map of Rome

What had his life been like before?

What did he risk by leaving?

Do you think it was a good risk to take? Why or why not?

What do you think happened when he arrived in Rome?

PREPARE AND SPEAK

A. **GATHER IDEAS** Think about the experience of the speaker in the Consider the Ideas activity above. Have you had a similar experience? What risks in your own life do you feel were good to take? Make a list.

_____

_____

_____

B. **ORGANIZE IDEAS** Choose one risk from your list in Activity A. Prepare to talk about it. Use the outline to help you organize your ideas.

The risk you took: _____

The reason why you took this risk:

_____

_____

_____

_____

_____

Describe what happened:

_____

_____

_____

_____

_____

_____

_____

_____

What did you learn or gain from this experience?

_____

_____

_____

_____

_____

_____

C. SPEAK Give a one-minute presentation to your group or class about a risk you have taken. Refer to the Self-Assessment checklist below before you begin.

1. Use an appropriate phrase to introduce your topic.

2. Use your notes from Activity B to help you, but do not read exactly what you wrote.

3. Try to talk continuously for the entire minute.

iQ ONLINE Go online for your alternate Unit Assignment.

CHECK AND REFLECT

A. CHECK Think about the Unit Assignment as you complete the Self-Assessment checklist.

SELF-ASSESSMENT		
Yes	**No**	
☐	☐	I was able to speak easily about the topic.
☐	☐	My group or class understood me.
☐	☐	I used vocabulary from the unit.
☐	☐	I used the past perfect and simple past.
☐	☐	I used contractions of *had*.
☐	☐	I used phrases to introduce my topic, explain the order of events, and give reasons for events.

B. REFLECT Go to the Online Discussion Board to discuss these questions.

1. What is something new you learned in this unit?

2. Look back at the Unit Question—What risks are good to take? Is your answer different now than when you started this unit? If yes, how is it different? Why?

TRACK YOUR SUCCESS

Circle the words and phrases you have learned in this unit.

Nouns
audience 🔑
credit 🔑 AWL
debt 🔑
funds 🔑 AWL
income 🔑 AWL
invention 🔑
model 🔑
mystery 🔑
reputation 🔑

Verbs
discover 🔑
embarrass 🔑
expose 🔑 AWL
investigate 🔑 AWL
locate 🔑 AWL
promote 🔑 AWL
prove 🔑
publish 🔑 AWL
retire 🔑
solve 🔑
threaten 🔑

Adjectives
financial 🔑 AWL
previous 🔑 AWL

Phrases
I'm going to talk
    about …
I want to talk about …
in order to
My topic is …
This presentation is
    on …

🔑 Oxford 3000™ words
AWL Academic Word List

Check (✓) the skills you learned. If you need more work on a skill, refer to the page(s) in parentheses.

NOTE TAKING ☐	I can use a chart to separate risks and outcomes. (p. 103)
LISTENING ☐	I can identify amounts and cardinal and ordinal numbers. (pp. 109–110)
VOCABULARY ☐	I can use word families. (p. 115)
GRAMMAR ☐	I can use the past perfect. (p. 117)
PRONUNCIATION ☐	I can use the contraction of *had*. (p. 119)
SPEAKING ☐	I can give a short presentation. (p. 120)
UNIT OBJECTIVE ▶▶▶▶ ☐	I can gather information and ideas to give a short presentation on a risk I have taken.

LISTENING	▶	inferring a speaker's attitude
VOCABULARY	▶	using the dictionary
GRAMMAR	▶	gerunds and infinitives as the objects of verbs
PRONUNCIATION	▶	stress on important words
SPEAKING	▶	leading a group discussion
NOTE TAKING	▶	building an outline to take notes on a discussion

UNIT QUESTION

Are we responsible for the world we live in?

A Discuss these questions with your classmates.

1. What does "to take responsibility" mean?

2. Do you think you are a responsible citizen?

3. Look at the photo. What are these people doing? Why?

B Listen to *The Q Classroom* online. Then answer these questions.

1. What three ways are mentioned as ways in which people can be responsible in their communities? Which of these things do you do? Which don't you do? Why not?

2. Felix says it is "not realistic to expect everyone to do those things" as they don't have time. Do you agree?

iQ ONLINE　**C** Go online to watch a video about TOMS Shoes. Then check your comprehension.

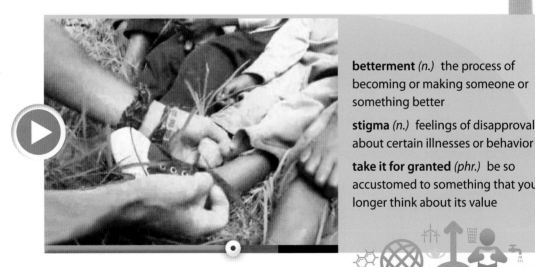

betterment *(n.)* the process of becoming or making someone or something better

stigma *(n.)* feelings of disapproval about certain illnesses or behavior

take it for granted *(phr.)* be so accustomed to something that you no longer think about its value

VIDEO VOCABULARY

iQ ONLINE　**D** Go to the Online Discussion Board to discuss the Unit Question with your classmates.

127

E Complete the web survey. Then work with a partner. Discuss who you think should be responsible for each activity.

www.rolesandresponsibilities.survey   Search

ROLES *and* RESPONSIBILITIES

Who should be responsible for...

picking up litter: _____

reducing traffic accidents: _____

recycling used
bottles, paper, etc: _____

fighting crime: _____

making sure
children go to school: _____

taking care of the elderly: _____

Parents
Children
Individuals
Government
Volunteer groups
Charities
Other

F Work in a group. Discuss your ideas from Activity E. Give reasons for your answers. Then discuss how responsible you personally feel for each activity. Give examples of ways you take responsibility.

LISTENING

LISTENING 1 | Corporate Social Responsibility

You are going to listen to a lecture to a group of business students. As you listen to the lecture, gather information and ideas about responsibility in the world we live in.

PREVIEW THE LISTENING

A. **PREVIEW** The lecturer starts by defining "corporate social responsibility" and then discusses its importance in today's world. What do you think "corporate social responsibility" means? Discuss your ideas with a partner. Take notes on your discussion.

_____

_____

_____

_____

B. **VOCABULARY** Read aloud these words from Listening 1. Check (✓) the ones you know. Use a dictionary to define any new or unknown words. Then discuss with a partner how the words will relate to the unit.

benefit *(n.)* 🔑	**fine** *(n.)*
consumer *(n.)* 🔑	**ignore** *(v.)* 🔑
demand *(v.)* 🔑	**impact** *(n.)* 🔑
developed *(adj.)*	**pollute** *(v.)*
fair *(adj.)* 🔑	**profit** *(n.)* 🔑

🔑 Oxford 3000™ words

iQ ONLINE **C.** Go online to listen and practice your pronunciation.

WORK WITH THE LISTENING

A. **LISTEN AND TAKE NOTES** Listen to the lecture. As you listen, complete the notes.

> CSR is the belief that companies need to be responsible for the
>
> _____, social, and _____ impact of their actions.
>
> Problems
>
> - Child employment: No. of children working: _____ million
>
> (Reasons: They learn quickly and are _____.) dangerous conditions/no health care
>
> - Pollution of rivers/oceans
>
> Pressure for change
>
> Consumers: demanding that workers get a _____
>
> Workers: expect companies to protect their _____ /
>
> maybe provide _____, etc.
>
> _____: demanding companies reduce pollution
>
> Who is responsible?
>
> - international companies   - local _____
>
> - individual managers   - _____
>
> Important to realize that _____ and responsibility can go together.

B. Read the statements. Write *T* (true) or *F* (false) according to what the professor says.

_____ 1. These days, more people are concerned about the impact companies have on the world we live in.

_____ 2. The issue of corporate social responsibility affects only a small number of people.

_____ 3. Companies in developed countries act more responsibly than those in developing countries.

_____ 4. Pressure on companies to act more responsibly comes mainly from governments.

_____ 5. It's often difficult to decide who is responsible for the actions of a company.

_____ 6. It's not possible for companies to be socially responsible and to make a profit.

C. Read the sentences. Then listen again. Circle the answer that best completes each statement.

1. The professor says it's understandable that companies _____.
   a. want to make a profit
   b. find it difficult to be socially responsible

2. He adds that people in developed countries don't seem to be concerned about _____.
   a. the conditions of workers elsewhere
   b. the price they pay for products

3. He suggests that consumers are beginning to _____.
   a. demand that governments do more to help
   b. realize they can help change the situation

4. The professor thinks that it is not easy to decide who _____.
   a. is to blame for the problems
   b. should take more responsibility

5. He thinks that stopping child labor is something that _____.
   a. can be achieved soon
   b. we are all responsible for

D. What two ways does the professor say companies can be forced to behave more responsibly?

iQ ONLINE **E. Go online to listen to** _Buy One, Give One_ **and check your comprehension.**

Vocabulary
Skill Review

In Unit 4, you learned to identify meaning from context. Remember to read the whole sentence and consider the **context**. This can help you identify the correct word and meaning.

F. VOCABULARY Use the new vocabulary from Listening 1. Complete each sentence with the correct word from the box.

benefit (n.)	**developed** (adj.)	**profit** (n.)	**fair** (adj.)	**impact** (n.)
consumer (n.)	**demand** (v.)	**fine** (n.)	**ignore** (v.)	**pollute** (v.)

1. As a(n) _____, I always try to buy products from companies I know well.

 | Listening and Speaking   **131**

2. Most people agree that companies should pay their workers a(n)

_____ wage.

3. There are laws protecting workers. Most companies follow these laws, but some companies _____ them.

4. The company accepted responsibility for the accident and paid a large

_____.

5. Some companies only care about money. Making a(n)

_____ is more important to them than anything else.

6. Private health care is just one _____ that some companies give their workers.

7. Angry workers around the world are starting to _____ more rights.

8. I think companies that _____ rivers with chemicals should be closed down.

9. People these days are more aware of the _____ of pollution on the environment.

10. _____ countries have a responsibility to help the global community.

iQ ONLINE **G.** Go online for more practice with the vocabulary.

SAY WHAT YOU THINK

Discuss the questions in a group.

Tip for Success

In discussion activities, always try to use words you have studied in the unit. This will help you learn the words and remember them in the future.

1. How important is it for companies to be socially responsible? What are the benefits?

2. Who do you think is more responsible for the actions of a company: the company itself or the individual decision-makers?

You can learn a lot about **a speaker's attitude** by noticing the way he talks. Someone who speaks slowly or sometimes hesitates before speaking might be nervous. Someone who raises her voice could be angry. Someone who is bored or uninterested might speak in a low voice with level intonation.

Listen to this excerpt from the lecture. Notice that the professor raises his voice. This indicates he feels passionately about the topic and is perhaps a little angry.

> We are all happy to buy our clothes more cheaply, but do we stop to think where they were made, and who made them?

Listen to this conversation. Notice that Speaker A speaks in a low voice with level intonation, expressing a lack of interest. Speaker B speaks slowly and hesitates. This shows he is nervous.

> **A:** It's the neighbor again. What does he want this time?
> **B:** Excuse me. Would you mind turning down the TV, please?
> **A:** Yeah, sure.

A. Listen to these sentences. Match each sentence with the speaker's attitude.

____ 1. Did you know that this is a nonsmoking area?   a. uninterested

____ 2. I don't know why Simon's always late for work.   b. angry

____ 3. Yeah. That garbage has been there for a week.   c. nervous

B. Listen to each conversation. Check (✓) the word that describes how the woman feels.

1. ☐ uninterested   ☐ angry   ☐ nervous
2. ☐ uninterested   ☐ angry   ☐ nervous
3. ☐ uninterested   ☐ angry   ☐ nervous

C. Work with a partner. Take turns reading the sentences. Practice sounding angry, uninterested, or nervous. Your partner will try to identify how you feel.

1. Someone's left the front door open again.

2. I think there's something wrong with the engine.

3. Muna hasn't finished the report yet.

iQ ONLINE **D.** Go online for more practice with inferring a speaker's attitude.

LISTENING 2 | Personal Responsibility

You are going to listen to an excerpt from a college seminar. As you listen to the excerpt, gather information and ideas about responsibility in the world we live in.

PREVIEW THE LISTENING

A. **PREVIEW** The students are discussing the issue of personal responsibility. Before you listen, think about the things you are responsible for in your daily life. Note your ideas, and then share them with the class.

B. **VOCABULARY** Read aloud these words from Listening 2. Check (✓) the ones you know. Use a dictionary to define any new or unknown words. Then discuss with a partner how the words will relate to the unit.

appropriate *(adj.)* 🔑	**influence** *(v.)* 🔑
check up on *(phr. v.)*	**lie** *(v.)* 🔑
guilty *(adj.)* 🔑	**obligation** *(n.)*
help out *(phr. v.)*	**sensible** *(adj.)* 🔑
in charge of *(phr.)*	**trust** *(v.)* 🔑

🔑 Oxford 3000™ words

 C. Go online to listen and practice your pronunciation.

WORK WITH THE LISTENING

A. **LISTEN AND TAKE NOTES** Listen to the first part of a seminar on personal responsibility. Note the examples each student gives of ways in which they take individual responsibility at home.

Name	Notes
Naomi	
Michael	
Nina	
Mark	

B. Circle the answer that best completes each statement.

1. (All / Some) of the students feel it is important to help out at home.

2. Naomi's parents (help with / don't care about) recycling.

3. Michael helps out around the house (every day / only on Saturdays).

4. Nina usually (does all the cooking / helps in the evenings).

5. Mark takes care of his (little sister / pets).

C. Listen to the rest of the seminar. Circle the answer that best completes each statement.

1. _____ of the students say their parents always want to know where they are.
   a. All   b. Many   c. None

2. The students seem to be _____ that their parents check up on them.
   a. pleased   b. annoyed   c. proud

3. The students feel their parents don't _____ them enough.
   a. trust   b. listen to   c. support

4. According to the professor, the amount of responsibility parents give their children might depend on their _____.
   a. behavior   b. attitude   c. age

5. The students do not _____ at what age children are responsible.
   a. know   b. agree   c. understand

D. Complete the sentences.

1. Mark says his parents _____ him a lot when he is out.

2. Neil once _____ to his parents, but regretted it later.

3. Naomi thinks that anyone from the age of _____ is responsible for his or her actions.

4. According to Mark, teenagers need to be protected from the wrong _____.

5. Michael says it is possible for young children to learn to _____ other people.

E. What two reasons does Neil give to explain why his parents don't like him playing video games? Does he think his parents are right to be worried? What's your opinion?

F. **VOCABULARY** Use the new vocabulary from Listening 2. Read the sentences. Then write each bold word or phrase next to the correct definition.

1. My mother told me it's not **appropriate** to wear torn jeans to the event.

2. Amy's parents worry, so they always **check up on** her.

3. Sometimes I feel **guilty** when I don't tell my parents where I'm going.

4. My parents are always busy, so I'm glad to **help out** around the house.

5. Who is **in charge of** health and safety in your school?

6. You shouldn't let other people **influence** you all the time. You need to make your own decisions.

7. Do you agree it's wrong to **lie**, even if the truth can hurt?

8. A teacher's main **obligation** is to help students learn.

9. It's not very **sensible** to run across a busy road.

10. It's important to have good friends you can **trust**.

a. _____ (phr. v.) to make sure someone is behaving well

b. _____ (v.) to believe someone is honest and reliable

c. _____ (adj.) responsible for doing something wrong

d. _____ (adj.) showing the ability to act in a reasonable way

e. _____ (v.) to have an effect on

f. _____ (n.) something that you must do because it is your duty or because you promised to do it

g. _____ (v.) to say something that you know is not true

h. _____ (phr.) responsible for something

i. _____ (phr. v.) to assist by doing useful jobs

j. _____ (adj.) suitable or right for a particular situation, person, or use

iQ ONLINE **G.** Go online for more practice with the vocabulary.

SAY WHAT YOU THINK

A. Discuss the questions in a group.

1. How much responsibility does your family give you? Are you content with this much responsibility?

2. At what age do you think someone becomes responsible for his or her actions (for example, behaving well in public, doing chores, or handling money)? Explain.

B. Think about the unit video, Listening 1, and Listening 2 as you discuss the questions.

1. What should companies do to protect the environment? In what ways should individuals be responsible for the environment? Who has more responsibility?

2. In what ways do you take responsibility for the world you live in? Give examples.

Vocabulary Skill | **Using the dictionary**

Finding the correct meaning

Words listed in a dictionary often have several meanings. To choose the correct meaning, first identify the part of speech (*noun*, *verb*, *adjective*, etc.). Then read all the definitions and example sentences. Finally, choose the meaning that best matches the context.

For example, read this conversation.

Nour: Look, May. I found this gold ring in the park. It fits me perfectly!

May: You're not going to keep it, are you? That's wrong! Turn it in to the police.

W*rong* can be a verb, noun, adjective, or adverb. Here, *wrong* is an adjective. W*rong (adj.)* in this dictionary has four different meanings. By considering the context and comparing examples, you will find that the most appropriate definition is Number 4—"not good or right."

> **wrong**[1] /rɔŋ/ *adj.* **1** not true or not correct; not right: *the wrong answer* ♦ *You have the wrong number* (= on the telephone). ♦ *I think you're wrong about that.* **ANT right 2** not the best; not suitable: *That's the wrong way to hold the bat.* ♦ *I think she married the wrong man.* **ANT right 3** (not before a noun) **wrong (with sb/sth)** causing problems or difficulties; not as it should be: *You look upset. Is something wrong?* ♦ *What's wrong with the car this time?* ♦ *She has something wrong with her leg.* **4 wrong (to do sth)** bad or against the law; not good or right: *It's wrong to tell lies.* ♦ *The man said that he had done nothing wrong.*

All dictionary entries are from the *Oxford American Dictionary for learners of English* © Oxford University Press 2011.

A. Read the sentences. Use a dictionary. Follow the steps in the Vocabulary Skill box on page 137 to identify the correct meaning of each bold word. Then write the definition.

1. People living in a **just** society should respect the law.

   (adjective) fair and right, reasonable

2. Complaints against dishonest politicians have reached a **peak** in the last few years.

   _____

3. If it doesn't stop raining soon, I think we should **abandon** the idea of going for a walk.

   _____

4. I don't have **outstanding** bills. I paid them all on Wednesday.

   _____

5. People in positions of authority shouldn't **abuse** their power.

   _____

6. Terri lives a very **moral** life. She's a good example for her children.

   _____

7. Companies that continue to pollute the environment **risk** getting heavy fines.

   _____

8. In any relationship, it's important to be **open** and supportive.

   _____

B. Choose five words from Activity A and write your own sentences in your notebook. Then compare your sentences with a partner.

 C. Go online for more practice using the dictionary.

SPEAKING

UNIT OBJECTIVE

At the end of this unit, you will take part in a group discussion. Make sure to take turns leading the group discussion.

Grammar | Gerunds and infinitives as the objects of verbs

A **gerund** is **the base form of the verb + -ing**. Gerunds can be used as the objects of certain verbs, e.g., *admit, avoid, discuss, dislike, enjoy, finish, miss, quit*.

> Nigel enjoys **doing** the chores.
> After she left home, Emily missed **seeing** her family.

An **infinitive** is *to* + **the base form of the verb**. Infinitives can also be used as the objects of certain verbs, e.g., *agree, choose, decide, hope, learn, need, plan, want*.

> Managers decided **to ignore** safety concerns.
> The company plans **to reduce** pollution by 10 percent over the next year.

Some verbs can be followed by either a gerund or an infinitive, with no difference in meaning, e.g., *begin, hate, like, love, prefer*.

> Workers at the factory began **demanding** better conditions and more pay.
> Workers at the factory began **to demand** better conditions and more pay.

A. Circle the correct verb forms to complete the conversation. If both the infinitive and the gerund are possible, circle both answers. Then practice the conversation with a partner.

Vicky: Hey, Janice. Did you hear the news? My boss agreed (<u>giving / to give</u>) me a promotion last month.

1

Janice: That's great! Well done, Vicky. So, now your life is all about work, work, work, right?

Vicky: Yeah, but I hope (<u>to become / becoming</u>) vice president next year. Are

2
you sorry you left the company?

Janice: Of course not! I love (<u>staying / to stay</u>) at home with my daughter. I don't

3
miss (<u>working / to work</u>) in an office at all.

4

Vicky: Hmm. I can't believe you chose (<u>quitting / to quit</u>). I thought you

wanted (<u>to stay / staying</u>) at the company for at least five more years.

Janice: Well, I did! But when I became a mother my priorities changed, I guess.

I felt I needed (<u>to spend / spending</u>) time at home with my daughter. My

husband and I have saved a lot of money, so I don't need (<u>having / to have</u>)

a job right now.

B. Write answers to the questions. Then discuss your answers with a partner.

1. Do you think a mother should quit working to look after her child?

_____

2. At what age would you want to become a parent?

_____

3. Do you think parents miss looking after their children after they leave home?

_____

4. How responsible do children need to feel for their parents when they are elderly?

_____

C. Go online for more practice with gerunds and infinitives as the objects of verbs.

D. Go online for the grammar expansion.

Speakers usually put more **stress** on the important words in a sentence, such as *nouns*, *verbs*, *adjectives*, and *adverbs*. These words are usually louder and clearer than other words in the sentence. Listening for stressed words can help you hear and understand the most important information.

Listen to this extract from Listening 1. Notice how the speaker stresses the important words.

> **We** are all **happy** to **buy** our **clothes** more **cheaply**, but do we **stop** to **think**
> **where** they were **made**, and **who made** them? Do you **know** who **made** your
> **jeans**, your **shirt**, or your **running shoes**?

A. Listen to more sentences from Listening 1. Underline the stressed words.

1. Corporate social responsibility is becoming a big issue these days.

2. Of course, companies want to make money. There's nothing wrong with that.

3. What is the cost to us, the planet, and the society we live in?

4. Imagine a company is polluting the environment. Who is responsible?

5. More and more consumers are demanding that companies pay their workers a fair wage.

B. Listen again. Repeat the sentences. Practice stressing the important words.

C. Read the extract below. Underline the important words that should be stressed. Then listen and check your answers.

As consumers demand higher standards, more companies are trying to improve the lives of their workers and the society they live in. These companies show that profit, and social responsibility, can go together.

D. Listen again. Then read the extract aloud. Practice stressing the words you underlined in Activity C.

iQ ONLINE **E.** Go online for more practice with word stress.

When discussing a topic in a group, it is important to choose one person to **lead the discussion**. The role of the leader is to guide the flow of the discussion. The leader

- starts the discussion
- gets comments from the members of the group
- keeps the discussion on topic
- ends the discussion

Here are some phrases you can use when you are leading a discussion.

Starting the discussion

The topic I'd like to discuss today is …
Today, we're going to discuss …
Our topic today is …

Getting comments from different people

What do you think, Massoud?
Kelly, what's your opinion?
Do you have anything to add, Charlene?

Keeping on topic

I think we need to return to the topic. What is your view on …?
Sorry, but can we keep to the topic?
Let's get back on topic.

Ending the discussion

That's all we have time for today.
To sum up, then, (summarize the main points)

A. Listen to this excerpt from a discussion on recycling. Complete the discussion with the phrases you hear. Then practice the discussion in a group of four.

Leader: OK, so today _____ recycling, and exactly

          ₁

who should be responsible. Brad, _____?

                    ₂

Brad: Well, I think that basically as individuals we can't change much. It's the government that has to take action.

Leader: I see. _____, Seline?

             ₃

Seline: I don't agree. We all need to do what we can. I mean, just one person can't do much … but everyone in the world acting together can change a lot! It's the same with raising money for charity. When everyone gives a little money, you can raise millions!

Brad: Yes. My brother ran a marathon for charity last year and …

Leader: Sorry, but _____? Susan,

                   ₄

_____?

    ₅

Susan: Well, I probably agree with Brad. Recycling is such a big problem— you need the government to act, really.

Leader: OK, so _____, Susan and Brad feel the

                 ₆

government should take responsibility, while Seline thinks individuals should lead the way.

B. Work with a partner. Continue the discussion from Activity A, using your own ideas.

C. Go online for more practice leading a group discussion.

Building an outline is an effective way to take notes on a discussion. An outline is useful if you need to take comprehensive notes, as it will help you to make sure you cover all the main points. It will also show you how the different points relate to each other, as well as allow you to record examples and opinions in a systematic way.

To organize your notes in outline form, list the main points and then use indentation to record supporting points, opinions, and examples.

A. Study this outline from the discussion on recycling between Brad, Susan, and Seline. Notice how the main points and the details of their discussion are noted, along with their supporting ideas.

Topic   Who is responsible for recycling?

(main point) • *The government should be responsible*

(opinion) individuals can't change a lot

(opinion) it's a big problem so the government should act

(main point) • *Individuals should take responsibility*

(opinion) people must act together

(supporting idea) raising money for charity – a little money from a lot of people = $ $ $

B. With a partner, think back to your discussion on recycling in Activity B on page 143. Add any additional opinions and supporting details or examples to the outline above.

C. Listen again to Listening 2. Complete this outline on the discussion.

(Topic) *Individual responsibility*

(main point) • *Children should help out at home*

(example) *take out* _____

(example) *sort recycling*

(opinion) *recycling is* _____

(example) *do dishes*

(example) *wash* _____

(example) *look after* _____

(example) *take care of pets*

(main point) • *Parents should be responsible for their children*

(example) *know where their children are*

(example) _____ *them when they go out*

(opinion) *parents should* _____ *their children*

(main point) • *Children should not lie to their parents*

(example) *should be truthful about what they are doing*

(supporting idea) *feel* _____ *if lie*

(main point) • *Individual responsibility depends on age*

(opinion) *should know right from wrong at 16*

(opinion) *only responsible at 20*

(supporting idea) *at 16 can be easily* _____

(opinion) *responsible from 5 or 6*

(supporting idea) *possible to behave well/* _____ *others*

D. Go online for more practice building an outline to take notes on a discussion.

In this assignment, you are going to take part in a group discussion. As you prepare for the group discussion, think about the Unit Question, "Are we responsible for the world we live in?" Use information from Listening 1, Listening 2, the unit video, and your work in this unit to support your discussion. Refer to the Self-Assessment checklist on page 148.

CONSIDER THE IDEAS

Work in a group. Make a list of issues that affect your world (for example, pollution, crime, use of the Internet, etc.). Write your responsibilities concerning these issues below.

_____

_____

_____

_____

_____

PREPARE AND SPEAK

A. GATHER IDEAS Read the statements. Check (✓) the ones you agree with.

☐ Individuals, not governments, are responsible for the society we live in.
☐ The content and use of the Internet need to be controlled.
☐ Global warming is something that only governments can fight effectively.
☐ Responsibility to your family is more important than anything else.
☐ It is OK for parents to spy on their children.
☐ Stealing is always wrong.
☐ We should all give money to support charities.

B. **ORGANIZE IDEAS** Choose two statements from Activity A that you agree with and one that you disagree with. Complete the outline to help you prepare to give your opinion.

Agree

Statement: _____

Reasons: _____

_____

_____

Agree

Statement: _____

Reasons: _____

_____

_____

Disagree

Statement: _____

Reasons: _____

_____

_____

 for Success

When taking part in a group discussion, encourage other speakers by paying close attention. You might also want to take notes of any good ideas.

C. **SPEAK** Have a group discussion about whether or not we are responsible for the world we live in. Refer to the Self-Assessment checklist on page 148 before you begin.

1. Choose a leader for your discussion. The leader can begin the discussion by asking about your responses to the statements in Activity A.

2. When an issue you have written about in Activity B comes up for discussion, give your opinion and explain your reasons.

3. You can refer to your notes, but do not read exactly what you wrote.

4. Give each student a turn as group leader.

 Go online for your alternate Unit Assignment.

CHECK AND REFLECT

A. CHECK Think about the Unit Assignment as you complete the Self-Assessment checklist.

SELF-ASSESSMENT		
Yes	No	
☐	☐	I was able to speak easily about the topic.
☐	☐	My group understood me.
☐	☐	I used vocabulary from the unit.
☐	☐	I put stress on important words as I spoke.
☐	☐	I led a group discussion.
☐	☐	I used an outline to take notes on the discussion.

B. REFLECT Go to the Online Discussion Board to discuss these questions.

1. What is something new you learned in this unit?

2. Look back at the Unit Question—Are we responsible for the world we live in? Is your answer different now than when you started this unit? If yes, how is it different? Why?

TRACK YOUR SUCCESS

Circle the words and phrases you have learned in this unit.

Nouns
benefit 🔑 AWL
consumer 🔑 AWL
fine
impact 🔑 AWL
obligation
peak 🔑
profit 🔑

Verbs
abandon 🔑 AWL
abuse 🔑
demand 🔑
ignore 🔑 AWL
influence 🔑
lie 🔑
pollute
risk 🔑
trust 🔑

Adjectives
appropriate 🔑 AWL
developed
fair 🔑
guilty 🔑
just
moral 🔑
open 🔑
outstanding 🔑
sensible 🔑
wrong 🔑

Phrasal Verbs
check up on
help out

Phrases
Do you have anything
  to add?
in charge of
I think we need to
  return to the topic.
Let's get back on topic.
Our topic today is …
Sorry, but can we keep
  to the topic?
That's all we have time
  for today.
The topic I'd like to
  discuss today is …
To sum up, then,
Today, we're going to
  discuss …
What do you think?

🔑 Oxford 3000™ words
AWL Academic Word List

Check (✓) the skills you learned. If you need more work on a skill, refer to the page(s) in parentheses.

LISTENING ☐	I can infer a speaker's attitude. (p. 133)
VOCABULARY ☐	I can use a dictionary to find the correct meanings of words. (p. 137)
GRAMMAR ☐	I can use gerunds and infinitives as the objects of verbs. (p. 139)
PRONUNCIATION ☐	I can put stress on important words. (p. 141)
SPEAKING ☐	I can lead a group discussion. (p. 142)
NOTE TAKING ☐	I can build an outline to take notes on a discussion. (p. 144)
UNIT OBJECTIVE ▶▶▶ ☐	I can gather information and ideas to state and explain my opinions about our responsibility for issues impacting our world.

LISTENING ▶ listening for signposts
VOCABULARY ▶ idioms
GRAMMAR ▶ types of sentences
PRONUNCIATION ▶ intonation in different types of sentences
SPEAKING ▶ agreeing and disagreeing
NOTE TAKING ▶ taking and organizing notes from a discussion

UNIT QUESTION

Can money buy happiness?

A Discuss these questions with your classmates.

1. How much money do you think people really need in order to be happy? Explain.

2. Do you think more money would make you happier? Why or why not?

3. Look at the photo. Would you be happier if you could buy a home like this? Why or why not?

B Listen to *The Q Classroom* online. Then answer these questions.

1. What things did the students mention they would do if they had more money?

2. According to Felix, what is something money can't buy?

iQ ONLINE   **C** Go to the Online Discussion Board to discuss the Unit Question with your classmates.

Listen to a presentation and an interview and gather information and ideas to participate in a group discussion evaluating the influence money has on happiness.

D Complete the questionnaire.

One Million Dollars

Imagine someone gives you one million dollars. Rank the following expenses in order of their importance to you, from 1 (most important) to 10 (least important).

☐ more education

☐ a new car

☐ a new house

☐ new clothes

☐ travel

☐ giving money to charity

☐ helping friends or family

☐ a flat-screen TV

☐ a vacation home

☐ paying off debt

E Now compare your answers with a partner. Discuss the similarities and differences in your choices.

F Write the three things that make you the happiest. Then compare this list with the three things you chose in the questionnaire in Activity D. With your partner, discuss which list of things makes you happier and why.

_____

_____

_____

LISTENING

LISTENING 1 | Sudden Wealth

UNIT OBJECTIVE

You are going to listen to a presentation on how people can change when they suddenly become rich. As you listen to the presentation, gather information and ideas about money and happiness.

PREVIEW THE LISTENING

A. **PREVIEW** Which topics do you think will be presented? Check (✓) your ideas.

☐ how sudden wealth makes people happy

☐ how sudden wealth causes problems

☐ the advantages and disadvantages of sudden wealth

Tip for Success

A question and answer early in a talk often indicates the speaker's main topic.

B. **VOCABULARY** Read aloud these words from Listening 1. Check (✓) the ones you know. Use a dictionary to define any new or unknown words. Then discuss with a partner how the words will relate to the unit.

acquire *(v.)* 🔑	**destructive** *(adj.)*	**immediate** *(adj.)* 🔑
circumstances *(n.)* 🔑	**dramatic** *(adj.)* 🔑	**pleasure** *(n.)* 🔑
complicated *(adj.)* 🔑	**get used to** *(phr.)*	**wear off** *(phr. v.)*

🔑 Oxford 3000™ words

iQ ONLINE

C. Go online to listen and practice your pronunciation.

WORK WITH THE LISTENING

A. **LISTEN AND TAKE NOTES** Listen to the presentation about sudden wealth. Take notes in the chart as you listen.

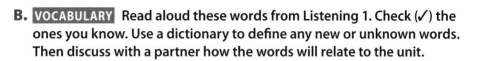

Sudden Wealth	
Positive effects	**Negative effects**

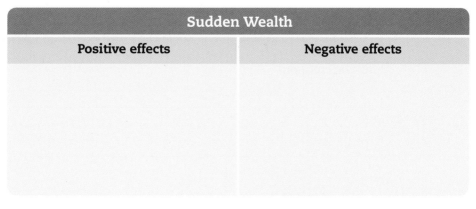

B. Read the statements. Write *T* (true) or *F* (false). Then correct each false statement to make it true. Explain your answer with information from the listening.

	Supporting information in the listening
_F_ 1. Getting rich suddenly often ~~reduces~~ stress. _{causes}	People who acquire a sudden fortune . . . experience a lot of stress.
____ 2. At first, acquiring a lot of money has a positive effect on our brains.	
____ 3. For most people, acquiring sudden wealth increases happiness.	
____ 4. Sudden wealth can cause many different problems.	
____ 5. People can feel more alone after they become suddenly wealthy.	

C. Listen again. Write two examples for each main point. Compare your ideas with a partner.

Effect on our brains

1. _____

2. _____

Effect on relationships

1. _____

2. _____

Effect on emotions

1. _____

2. _____

D. Read each situation. Based on the information in the listening, choose the best word or phrase to complete each sentence.

1. Mark got a great deal of money from his grandfather, but they didn't get along. Mark probably feels ____ .
   a. happy
   b. sad
   c. guilty

2. Elena received a very large bonus from her job. She bought a new car. After a month, she ____ .
   a. bought a new house
   b. opened a savings account
   c. gave the money away

3. Karen receives millions of dollars. She buys a house in an expensive town. After six months, she ____ .
   a. has all new friends
   b. misses her old friends
   c. feels supported in her new home

E. Read about a Canadian couple that suddenly received a lot of money. Answer the questions according to what you learned in the listening. Discuss your answers with a partner.

Allen and Violet Large received more than 11 million dollars in 2010. The Larges lived in Nova Scotia, Canada, and were in their 70s. Violet was getting treatment for cancer at the time. They didn't go on a spending spree. They decided to give their money away to family, charities, and even the hospital where Violet was treated. Married for 36 years, the Larges didn't need the money. Violet said, "What you never had, you never miss." As Allen said, "We have each other."

1. How do most people respond to receiving money? How did the Larges respond differently?

   _____

   _____

2. Would the Larges be happier if they spent the money? Why or why not?

   _____

   _____

F. **VOCABULARY** Use the new vocabulary from Listening 1. Read the paragraphs. Then fill in the blanks with the correct words from the box.

acquire (v.)	destructive (adj.)	immediate (adj.)
circumstances (n.)	dramatic (adj.)	pleasure (n.)
complicated (adj.)	get used to (phr.)	wear off (phr. v.)

A Success Story?

Thomas Carter never believed that he would _____
1
12 million dollars, but in 2004, that's exactly what happened. He didn't receive the money from his parents—he got it when he sold an antique vase from his attic. At the time, he only had $213 in his bank account. Tom's sudden wealth brought him a lot of _____, because he could buy whatever
2
he wanted. But this _____ improvement did not last long.
3
He started to change his life in significant ways. These _____
4
changes were hard for Tom to deal with, because everything in his life became so different. Within three months, Tom had spent almost all his millions on a restaurant, a used-car lot, and an airplane. His _____ had
5
changed, but he still had trouble managing his money.

Over the next eight years, many things started happening that Tom didn't understand. His life, which had once seemed simple, was becoming more and more _____. The effects of his wealth soon became
6
_____; it damaged many of his relationships with friends
7
and family members. Like many people who _____ spending
8
a lot of money, Tom couldn't stop even after he had lost so much of it. He continued to buy houses, cars, motorcycles, and boats. The good feeling he got from spending money started to _____ as time passed.
9
Tom told people later that he was happier before he made all that money.

iQ ONLINE **G.** Go online for more practice with the vocabulary.

SAY WHAT YOU THINK

Discuss the questions in a group.

1. Which of the effects mentioned in Listening 1 do you think are the most difficult to deal with? Why?

2. Has sudden money made anyone you know about happier or unhappier? Explain.

3. Under what circumstances do you think money could make someone happier?

Listening Skill **Listening for signposts**

Signposts are words and phrases that can tell you the order in which things happened. Listen for signposts to help you follow the order of events and the logic in a text.

Listen to these examples of signposts from Listening 1.

> **First**, it affects how our brains work, at least for a while.
> **In the beginning**, when we get the money, our brain identifies it as pleasure.
> **Then** that feeling wears off.

Here are some words and phrases which are used as signposts.

At the start	In the middle	At the end
At first,	After (that),	Finally,
First,	Before (that),	In conclusion,
In the beginning,	Later,	In summary,
	Next,	
	Second,	
	Then,	

A. Listen to a reporter interview a secretary who suddenly acquired a lot of money. Complete the interview with the signposts you hear.

Reporter: You are one of many people in this town who suddenly acquired a lot of wealth when your company was purchased by a large software company. How has that affected your life?

Laura Green: Well, _____ it was pretty incredible. It took a
                                    1
while for me to believe it. But _____ I began to realize what
                                              2
it could actually do to my life. Things have changed dramatically.

Reporter: In what way?

Laura: I paid off all of my credit card debt. And sent my son to college.
Receiving this money was just fantastic! _____, I was
                                                        3
worried all the time.

Reporter: So your financial circumstances have improved. What else
has changed?

Laura: You know, I was a secretary at that company for 20 years. I had gotten
used to just working to pay the bills. I always wished I could do more with
my life. _____ I can do that.
              4

Reporter: And what do you want to do?

Laura: _____, I'm going to go to Paris. I've always dreamed of
                    5
going there. _____, I'm thinking of going back to school. I'd
                          6
like to study gardening. I love flowers. _____, maybe I will
                                                    7
open my own business.

Reporter: We hear stories in the news all the time about people who get a
lot of money suddenly and have many problems. How do you think those
problems can be avoided?

Laura: It's about staying true to your values and remembering what's really
important in life. You don't need to let money complicate things.

B. Answer the questions using signposts and complete sentences. Then take turns asking and answering the questions with a partner.

1. What did Laura do before she received the money?

   Before that, she worked as a secretary.

2. How did Laura feel about the money in the beginning?

   _____

3. What is one of the first things she did with the money?

   _____

4. What did she do after that?

   _____

5. What is Laura going to do in the immediate future?

   _____

6. What will she do next?

   _____

iQ ONLINE **C.** Go online for more practice listening for signposts.

| **Happiness Breeds Success ... and Money!**

 **UNIT OBJECTIVE** ▶▶▶ You are going to listen to an interview with Sonja Lyubomirsky, a psychologist who does research on happiness. As you listen to the interview, gather information and ideas about money and happiness.

PREVIEW THE LISTENING

Sonja Lyubomirsky

A. **PREVIEW** Which topics do you think psychologist Sonja Lyubomirsky will discuss?

☐ hobbies   ☐ travel

☐ income   ☐ where people live

☐ relationships   ☐ work

B. **VOCABULARY** Read aloud these words from Listening 2. Check (✓) the ones you know. Use a dictionary to define any new or unknown words. Then discuss with a partner how the words will relate to the unit.

analysis *(n.)* 🔑	independence *(n.)* 🔑
associated with *(adj. + prep.)* 🔑	outcome *(n.)*
burn out *(phr. v.)*	persuasive *(adj.)*
conduct *(v.)* 🔑	somewhat *(adv.)* 🔑
demonstrate *(v.)* 🔑	wholly *(adv.)*

🔑 Oxford 3000™ words

iQ ONLINE **C.** Go online to listen and practice your pronunciation.

WORK WITH THE LISTENING

🔊 **A.** **LISTEN AND TAKE NOTES** Listen to the interview. Write the phrases in the correct boxes to complete the cause-effect chain.

more successful at job

• better work environment
• the happier we are
• higher income

1. How did Lyubomirsky's research influence her ideas about happiness?
   a. Her research proved that our personal relationships have the greatest influence on our happiness.
   b. Although she expected relationships to influence our happiness, her research showed that work was more important.
   c. Her research showed that wealth influenced happiness more than work.

2. What qualities in a job are associated with greater happiness?
   a. productivity, creativity, and independence
   b. structure, routine, and a pleasant environment
   c. friends, a high income, and good benefits

3. What is the relationship between happiness and income?
   a. The more money we have, the happier we will be.
   b. The happier we are, the less we care about money.
   c. Happiness, job satisfaction, and income influence each other in a positive way.

C. Read the statements. Write *T* (true) or *F* (false). Then correct each false statement to make it true.

_____ 1. Lyubomirsky and her colleagues looked at the research from 300 studies.

_____

_____ 2. Lyubomirsky has changed her ideas about what makes us happy.

_____

_____ 3. Our jobs have more of an effect on happiness than our personal relationships do.

_____

_____ 4. Happy people take fewer sick days than unhappy people.

_____

_____ 5. People who are happy when they are young will have lower salaries when they are older.

_____

_____ 6. Creativity and productivity at work leads to happier workers.

_____

D. Show the relationship between each pair. Use a plus sign (+) if there is a positive relationship, or a minus sign (–) if there is a negative relationship. Use Ø if there is no relationship between the two.

1. high creativity in a job   _+_ job satisfaction

2. a job that's the same every day   ___ job satisfaction

3. higher income   ___ happiness

4. happiness   ___ sick days

5. happiness   ___ burn out

6. happiness at 18   ___ quality of job at 26

7. happiness at 18   ___ size of apartment at 30

8. happiness at 21   ___ higher income at 37

E. Go online to listen to *Counterfeit Money* and check your comprehension.

Vocabulary Skill Review

In Unit 1, you learned that suffixes help you recognize parts of speech. Look at the sentences in Activity F. Underline the common suffixes that indicate nouns, verbs, adjectives, and adverbs.

F. **VOCABULARY** Use the new vocabulary from Listening 2. Read the sentences. Then write each bold word or phrase next to the correct definition.

1. The **analysis** of the research shows that money doesn't make people happier.

2. Sudden wealth is **associated with** stress. Many people who become rich quickly experience a lot of stress.

3. I have been working too much lately. I'm afraid I'm going to **burn out**.

4. The researchers are going to **conduct** a study on money and happiness. The study will involve fifty people.

5. Mia likes a job with **independence**. She doesn't like someone telling her what to do.

6. Researchers used the results of their study to **demonstrate** that more money does not make people happier.

7. One **outcome** of sudden wealth is a change in relationships. Others include stress and loneliness.

8. The salesman was very **persuasive**. I bought the first car he showed me!

9. I'm **somewhat** unhappy at work, but not so much that I plan to quit my job.

10. I was **wholly** to blame for the argument. You did nothing wrong.

a. _____ *(n.)* the state of being free and not controlled by another person

b. _____ *(adv.)* completely; fully

c. _____ *(v.)* to show clearly that something exists or is true; to prove something

d. _____ *(n.)* the careful examination of something

e. _____ *(phr. v.)* to become very tired through overwork

f. _____ *(v.)* to do, carry out, or organize something

g. _____ *(adj. + prep.)* connected to; involved with

h. _____ *(n.)* a result or effect of an action or event

i. _____ *(adj.)* able to make someone do or believe something

j. _____ *(adv.)* a little

iQ ONLINE | **G.** Go online for more practice with the vocabulary.

SAY WHAT YOU THINK

A. Discuss the questions in a group.

1. Which do you think comes first, happiness or money? Explain.

2. What qualities of a happy person do you think lead to better employment and financial outcomes?

B. Before you watch the video, discuss the questions in a group.

1. How much money or income do you think is necessary to be happy?

2. What are the best ways to help the poor?

iQ ONLINE | **C.** Go online to watch a video about how microloans, or very small loans, can help the poor. Then check your comprehension.

> **VIDEO VOCABULARY**
>
> **collateral** *(n.)* property or something valuable that you plan to give to someone if you cannot pay back money that you borrow
>
> **creditworthy** *(adj.)* able to be trusted to pay back money that is owed
>
> **hustle** *(v.)* sell something
>
> **profound** *(adj.)* very great
>
> **taken hold** *(phr.)* become strong
>
> **welfare** *(n.)* money the government pays regularly to people who are poor, sick, unemployed, etc.

Critical Thinking **Tip**

Question 1 of Activity D asks you to **choose** between two things. To make the best choice, you evaluate a variety of factors, including your knowledge and experience.

D. Think about the unit video, Listening 1, and Listening 2 as you discuss the questions.

1. What is the difference between sudden wealth and earning more money from a better job? Which would you prefer? Why?

2. How responsible do you think people are for their own wealth or lack of money? How much responsibility do the rich have to help the poor?

Vocabulary Skill   Idioms

Idioms are phrases that have a different meaning than the literal meanings of the individual words. Look at these examples.

> **Out of the blue**, Pauline found a plastic bottle.

Out of the blue means "unexpectedly." For example, storms from a clear blue sky are unexpected.

> Communicating with a new friend from another state **is a snap** these days, thanks to the Internet and e-mail.

To *be a snap* means "to be really easy." For example, making a *snapping* noise with your fingers is really easy.

Learning idioms is an important way to increase your vocabulary. English speakers use them often. As you become more familiar with idioms, you will be able to understand conversations, television programs, and radio broadcasts better.

A. Work with a partner. Read the sentences. Then match each bold phrase with the correct definition.

____ 1. I hope you have a great summer. **Drop me a line** sometime and tell me how you are doing.

____ 2. Mark seems very upset. I think he has something he needs to **get off his chest**.

____ 3. **Off the top of my head**, I don't have any ideas about what we should do.

____ 4. Sometimes I can't **hold my tongue**. I always want to say what I'm feeling.

____ 5. I'm **all ears**. How did your conversation with Professor Elliot go? I want to hear every detail!

a. listening carefully

b. without thinking first

c. to keep quiet; not to say anything

d. to talk about a problem

e. to write someone a letter

Tip for Success

If you know all the words in a phrase, but still don't understand the meaning, the phrase might be an idiom. Idioms have to be learned by experience.

B. Complete the conversations with the idioms from Activity A. Then practice the conversations with a partner.

1. **A:** I have to do a report. Where can I find out about languages that are dying out?

    B: Hmm. I don't know _____ but we can look online.

2. **A:** I can't _____ anymore. I just have to say something.

    B: That's probably not a good idea. I think you should keep quiet.

3. **A:** I can't wait for my vacation. I've never been to Australia.

    B: Oh, you'll have a great time. _____ when you can, so I know how your trip is going.

4. **A:** I have something really interesting to tell you.

    B: What is it? I'm _____ .

5. **A:** Listen, I've got something I've got to _____ . I'm really upset about it.

    B: What is it? Tell me what's wrong.

iQ ONLINE **C.** Go online for more practice using idioms.

Uluru, Australia

SPEAKING

UNIT OBJECTIVE ▶▶▶▶ At the end of this unit, you will participate in a group discussion evaluating the influence money has on happiness. Make sure to use appropriate phrases for agreeing and disagreeing when you discuss this topic.

Grammar | Types of sentences

In English, there are four main sentence types in normal speech.

Declarative sentence (a statement):	I am trying to save money.
Interrogative sentence (a question):	How do you save money?
Imperative sentence (a direction or command):	Save your money.
Exclamatory sentence (an exclamation):	I saved so much money!

Punctuation at the end of sentences

Use periods with declarative sentences, question marks with interrogative sentences, and exclamation marks with exclamatory sentences.

Imperative sentences can end with either a period or an exclamation mark. An exclamation mark shows more emotion.

A. Read the conversation. Write the sentence type (declarative, interrogative, imperative, exclamatory) next to each sentence. Then practice the conversation with a partner.

_____ 1. **Hong:** There are so many cars here!

_____ 2. **Nan:** Yeah, I know. It's hard to believe we can finally afford a new one.

_____ 3. **Hong:** I'm just glad we got the money as a reward for helping someone.

_____ 4. **Nan:** Me, too. I didn't even know your uncle very well.

_____ 5. **Hong:** Didn't you meet him at the wedding?

_____ 6. **Nan:** Yes, but I only had a short conversation with him.

_____ 7. **Hong:** I had no idea that he was going to give us so much money.

_____ 8. **Nan:** Speaking of money, hold my purse for a minute. I can't find my wallet!

B. Go online for more practice with sentence types.

C. Go online for the grammar expansion.

| **Intonation in different types of sentences**

Intonation varies according to **sentence type**. Learning intonation patterns can help you understand if a speaker is asking a question, giving a command, or making a statement.

Declarative and imperative sentences:

Declarative and imperative sentences have a falling intonation.

> I am going to purchase a new home.
>
> Please give me some advice.

Exclamatory sentences:

Exclamatory sentences have a rise-fall intonation.

> This is fun!

Interrogative sentences:

Remember that interrogative sentences or questions have two intonation patterns. *Yes/no* questions have a rising intonation pattern.

> Are you coming with me?

Wh- questions have a falling intonation pattern.

> Why did you leave?

 A. Listen to the sentences. Check (✓) the type of sentence for each according to the intonation you hear.

1. a. ☐ statement   ☐ *yes/no* question
   b. ☐ statement   ☐ *yes/no* question

2. a. ☐ command   ☐ *wh-* question
   b. ☐ command   ☐ *wh-* question

3. a. ☐ statement   ☐ exclamation
   b. ☐ statement   ☐ exclamation

B. Listen again. Repeat the sentences using the same intonation that you hear.

 **C.** Go online for more practice with intonation in different types of sentences.

There are certain phrases used for **agreeing and disagreeing**. It's important to know which phrases and expressions are appropriate for formal and informal situations. An informal conversation is very different from a formal discussion at college or at work.

Here are some phrases you can use when you want to agree or disagree in different situations.

Agreeing		Disagreeing
I agree (completely).	formal	I disagree.
That's exactly what I think.		I don't agree (at all).
That's a good point.		Sorry, but that's not my opinion.
That's right.		I don't feel the same way.
I think so too.		I don't think so.
Absolutely!		No way!
Yeah, I know!	informal	Oh, come on!

A. Listen to the conversations. Complete each conversation with the phrases you hear.

1. **Ellie:** What are you going to do with the money your grandfather gave you?

   Sam: I'm not sure. I think I'm going to take an expensive vacation.

   Ellie: Really? Don't you have a lot of school loans to pay?

   Sam: _____₁. Maybe the vacation's not such a good idea.

   Ellie: _____₂! Vacations are fun, but it's much more important to pay off your debt.

2. **Monica:** I think raising the average income in countries around the world is the best way to increase the level of happiness.

   Patricia: I _____₃. More money might make the very poor happier, but not everyone.

Monica: I _____. I think everyone except perhaps the very
        4
wealthy will benefit from a higher income.

Patricia: Well, I can see we'll just have to agree to disagree.

iQ ONLINE **B.** Go online for more practice with agreeing and disagreeing.

Note-taking Skill **Taking and organizing notes from a discussion**

Sometimes it is important to take notes from a pair or group discussion. You may
need to report on the discussion to the class, or you may want to use the ideas
from the discussion to prepare for a test, write an essay, or make a presentation.
One way to organize your notes is by using a graphic organizer. For a pair
discussion, you can use a Venn diagram. This allows you to show points of
agreement and disagreement.

A. With a partner, read this excerpt from a discussion about happiness.
   Then take notes in the Venn diagram on page 170.

Tom: OK. What do we want to say about the research on money and
happiness?

Marc: Well, according to the study by Betsey Stevenson and Jeffrey Wolfers,
richer people are happier. I know when I have more money, I feel more relaxed
about paying my bills.

Tom: True. But didn't research in the U.K. by Layard show that as long as you
have a certain amount, you can be happy? All I want is to be able to pay all
my bills and have some extra to do the things I enjoy. I don't need a really big
house or an expensive car.

Marc: I agree. I need a home and a car, but they don't have to be really huge
or expensive. But I do want to have enough money to travel. And when I say
travel, I mean, to places I've never been—like Chiang Mai in Thailand and
Machu Picchu in Peru. And I don't want to skimp. I want to really enjoy the
trip and stay in nice hotels.

Tom: Yeah, I would love to go to those places. But I don't need to stay in nice
hotels. I could camp or stay in hostels. The important thing is the people you
are with and the experiences you have.

Tom's ideas   **Both Tom and Marc agree**   **Marc's ideas**

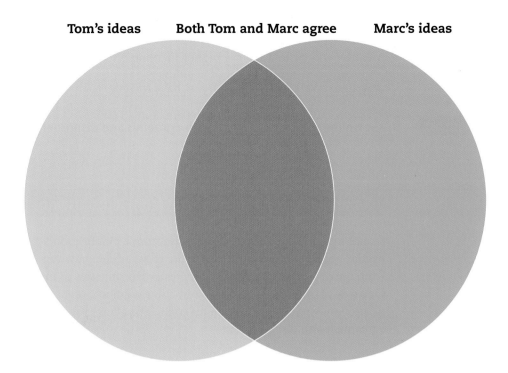

B. Use your notes to answer the questions.

1. What was the topic of the discussion? _____

2. What information did they give to support their ideas?

   _____

   _____

3. What did the two speakers agree about?

   _____

   _____

4. What did they disagree about?

   _____

   _____

C. With a partner, summarize the speakers' points using the notes from the graphic organizer.

iQ ONLINE **D.** Go online for more practice taking and organizing notes from a discussion.

In this assignment, you are going to take part in a group discussion about money and happiness. As you prepare for the discussion, think about the Unit Question, "Can money buy happiness?" Use information from Listening 1, Listening 2, the unit video, and your work in this unit to support your discussion. Refer to the Self-Assessment checklist on page 172.

CONSIDER THE IDEAS

Work with a partner. Discuss the questions about money and happiness. Be sure to use the correct intonation when you ask each other questions.

What is money's influence on happiness?

What kind of person do you think would be happier with more money? Why?

Would your life be different if you had more or less money? How?

Is it more enjoyable to give or receive money? Why?

PREPARE AND SPEAK

Tip for Success

When disagreeing with someone, you can sound more polite by starting with *I know what you mean, but …* or *I see your point, but …*

A. GATHER IDEAS Take notes on your discussion with your partner. Use these questions to guide you.

1. What were the main points of your discussion?

2. What did you agree on?

3. What did you disagree on?

B. ORGANIZE IDEAS Choose one question from the Consider the Ideas activity. Use the outline to help you prepare for a group discussion. Do not write exactly what you are going to say. Just write notes to help you organize your ideas.

Question: _____

Ideas that I agree with:

_____

_____

Ideas that I disagree with:

_____

_____

My answer to the question:

_____

_____

Reasons for my answer:

_____

_____

Examples:

_____

_____

C. SPEAK Work in a group. Take turns presenting your ideas on the questions you chose in Activity B. Refer to the Self-Assessment checklist below before you begin.

iQ ONLINE Go online for your alternate Unit Assignment.

CHECK AND REFLECT

A. CHECK Think about the Unit Assignment as you complete the Self-Assessment checklist.

		SELF-ASSESSMENT
Yes	**No**	
☐	☐	I was able to speak easily about the topic.
☐	☐	My group understood me.
☐	☐	I used vocabulary from the unit.
☐	☐	I used different types of sentences when speaking.
☐	☐	I used different intonation patterns.
☐	☐	I used phrases to agree and disagree.

B. REFLECT Go to the Online Discussion Board to discuss these questions.

1. What is something new you learned in this unit?

2. Look back at the Unit Question—Can money buy happiness? Is your answer different now than when you started this unit? If yes, how is it different? Why?

TRACK YOUR SUCCESS

Circle the words and phrases you have learned in this unit.

Nouns
analysis 🔑 AWL
circumstances 🔑 AWL
independence 🔑
outcome AWL
pleasure 🔑

Verbs
acquire 🔑 AWL
conduct 🔑 AWL
demonstrate 🔑 AWL
inherit

Adjectives
associated (with) 🔑
complicated 🔑
destructive
dramatic 🔑 AWL
immediate 🔑
persuasive

Adverbs
Absolutely! 🔑
Finally, 🔑 AWL
First, 🔑
Later, 🔑
Next, 🔑
Second, 🔑
somewhat 🔑 AWL
Then, 🔑
wholly

Phrasal Verbs
burn out
wear off

Phrases
After (that),
At first,
Before (that),
get used to

I agree (completely).
I disagree.
I don't agree (at all).
I don't feel the same way.
I don't think so.
I think so too.
In conclusion,
In summary,
In the beginning,
No way!
Oh, come on!
Sorry, but that's not my
   opinion.
That's a good point.
That's exactly what I
   think.
That's right.
Yeah, I know!

🔑 Oxford 3000™ words
AWL Academic Word List

Check (✓) the skills you learned. If you need more work on a skill, refer to the page(s) in parentheses.

LISTENING ■	I can listen for signposts. (p. 157)
VOCABULARY ■	I can use idioms. (p. 164)
GRAMMAR ■	I can use different types of sentences. (p. 166)
PRONUNCIATION ■	I can use correct intonation in different types of sentences. (p. 167)
SPEAKING ■	I can use phrases for agreeing and disagreeing. (p. 168)
NOTE TAKING ■	I can take and organize notes from a discussion. (p. 169)
UNIT OBJECTIVE ▶▶▶	■ I can gather information and ideas to participate in a group discussion evaluating the influence money has on happiness.

UNIT 8

Behavioral Science

LISTENING	▶	listening for examples
VOCABULARY	▶	prefixes
GRAMMAR	▶	simple past and present perfect
PRONUNCIATION	▶	varying intonation to maintain interest
SPEAKING	▶	asking for and giving clarification
NOTE TAKING	▶	taking notes with examples

UNIT QUESTION

What can we learn from success and failure?

A Discuss these questions with your classmates.

1. What are some of the different ways a person can be successful?

2. In what ways do you think you are successful?

3. Look at the photo. What is happening? In what ways can failure affect people?

B Listen to *The Q Classroom* online. Then answer these questions.

1. What types of success do the students mention? Do you agree or disagree with their ideas? Why?

2. Marcus thinks we learn more from our failures than our successes. What explanation does he give for this opinion? Do you agree?

iQ ONLINE **C** Go online to watch a video about a race car driver. Then check your comprehension.

blown away *(adj.)* impressed by someone or something

mayhem *(n.)* confusion

pit crews *(n.)* teams of people that work on race cars

tinker *(v.)* repair things

VIDEO VOCABULARY

iQ ONLINE **D** Go to the Online Discussion Board to discuss the Unit Question with your classmates.

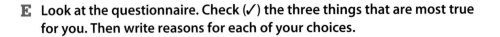

What Does Success Mean to You?

For Me Success Means ...	Reasons:
☐ being rich	
☐ doing well on exams	
☐ having a job I love	
☐ enjoying a happy family life	
☐ being able to do what I want	
☐ having lots of friends	
☐ enjoying good health	
☐ being famous	
☐ having a powerful or important job	
Your idea: _____	
Your idea: _____	

F Discuss your answers in a group. Explain the reasons for your choices.

LISTENING

You are going to listen to the beginning of a lecture by a college professor. As you listen to the lecture, gather information and ideas about what we can learn from success and failure.

PREVIEW THE LISTENING

A college professor is talking about the importance of success and what it means to be successful.

A. **PREVIEW** Which things do you think the college professor will say are important for success? Check (✓) your answers.

☐ being lucky

☐ having clear goals

☐ never giving up

☐ trying hard

B. **VOCABULARY** Read aloud these words from Listening 1. Check (✓) the ones you know. Use a dictionary to define any new or unknown words. Then discuss with a partner how the words will relate to the unit.

achieve *(v.)* 🔑	**goal** *(n.)* 🔑
determination *(n.)* 🔑	**measure** *(v.)* 🔑
downside *(n.)*	**realistic** *(adj.)* 🔑
frustrating *(adj.)*	**ruin** *(v.)* 🔑
give up *(phr. v.)*	**status** *(n.)* 🔑

🔑 Oxford 3000™ words

 C. Go online to listen and practice your pronunciation.

WORK WITH THE LISTENING

A. **LISTEN AND TAKE NOTES** Listen to the lecture. Complete the missing words in the chart, and add notes on any examples the professor gives.

Main points	Examples
1. Make sure your goals are _____.	
2. Aiming for success should not cause _____ or _____.	*none given*
3. Success can bring _____.	
4. Our definition of success changes with _____.	

B. In what ways does the professor use humor to make her points? Do you think this is an effective technique? Why or why not?

C. Listen to the lecture again. Circle the answer that best completes each statement according to what the professor says.

1. We learn that success is good _____.
   a. from an early age
   b. as we grow older

2. To be successful, you _____.
   a. need to set achievable goals
   b. should never stop trying to achieve your goals

3. Achieving your goals should be _____.
   a. the most important thing in your life
   b. one of several important things in your life

4. You should try to focus on _____.
   a. only the positive aspects of success
   b. both the positive and the negative aspects of success

5. You need to _____.
   a. keep the same goals throughout your life
   b. change your goals to match different stages in your life

D. Read the statements. Write *T* (true) or *F* (false). Then correct each false statements to make it true.

____ 1. This is the professor's first lecture on success to the class.

____ 2. She says that with hard work and determination, it is possible to achieve anything you want.

____ 3. According to the professor, trying to achieve some dreams can be a waste of time and effort.

____ 4. The professor says that trying too hard to be successful can cause problems.

____ 5. She argues that success can also bring failure.

____ 6. She says that people often see success differently as they grow older.

Vocabulary Skill Review

Remember to read the whole sentence and consider the *context*. This can help you identify the correct word and meaning.

E. **VOCABULARY** Use the new vocabulary from Listening 1. Read the sentences. Circle the answer that best matches the meaning of each bold word or phrase.

1. It may be difficult to **achieve** your dreams, but hard work can often help you get what you want from life.
   a. reach   b. control   c. remember

2. **Determination** is important for success. You have to keep trying even when it is difficult.
   a. force   b. willpower   c. luck

3. I love my job, but the **downside** is that the salary is low.
   a. mistake   b. error   c. disadvantage

4. It can be very **frustrating** to try hard without succeeding.
   a. difficult   b. boring   c. annoying

5. "If at first you don't succeed, try, try again." This saying means "don't **give up**".
   a. quit   b. fail   c. alter

6. Peter is a salesperson now, but his **goal** is to have his own business someday.
   a. argument   b. ambition   c. challenge

7. There are various ways to **measure** success. It's not just about making lots of money.
   a. judge   b. enjoy   c. discuss

8. It's not **realistic** to expect to be successful at everything you do. No one can be good at everything.
   a. confident   b. reasonable   c. intelligent

9. Don't wash that sweater in hot water. You'll **ruin** it.
   a. break   b. injure   c. spoil

10. Sarah's new job gave her a much higher **status** within the company.
   a. position   b. activity   c. popularity

 F. Go online for more practice with the vocabulary.

SAY WHAT YOU THINK

Discuss the questions in a group.

1. Do you agree with the points the professor makes about success? Why or why not?

2. Who is the most successful person you know? In what ways is he or she successful?

3. What things do you think are more important than success?

There are many different types of success.

Listening Skill Listening for examples

Listening for examples will help you understand a speaker's main points more clearly. Speakers often introduce examples with a common phrase that tells you that an example follows.

For example,	such as	To give (you) an example,
For instance,	Take, for example,	To illustrate this,

A. Listen to the lecture again. List the phrases the professor uses to introduce examples.

_____

_____

_____

_____

B. Listen to Paul talk about how his view of success has changed. List each example he gives. You do not need to write full sentences.

1. When he was younger, Paul says he was "money hungry."

   Example: _____

2. He also says he was concerned about status.

   Example: _____

3. These days, Paul says being successful for him means being healthy.

   Example: _____

4. He also says that having good friends is important to him.

   Example: _____

C. Think about one goal you would like to achieve. Write three benefits you expect from achieving this goal.

Your goal: _____

Benefits:

1. _____

   _____

2. _____

   _____

3. _____

   _____

D. Work with a partner. Take turns talking about your goals and their benefits. Use phrases from the Listening Skill box on page 180 when you give examples. Take notes below as you listen to your partner. Then discuss whether or not you agree with the benefits she or he expects.

Your partner's goal: _____

Benefits:

1. _____

   _____

2. _____

   _____

3. _____

   _____

 **E.** Go online for more practice listening for examples.

LISTENING 2 | The Benefits of Failure

UNIT OBJECTIVE ▶▶▶ You are going to listen to a short speech by a college student. As you listen to the speech, gather information and ideas about what we can learn from success and failure.

PREVIEW THE LISTENING

A. PREVIEW Carl Simmons, a college student, is talking about the opposite of success—failure. In what ways do you think failure can be a positive experience? Make a list of your ideas, and then compare with a partner.

_____

_____

B. **VOCABULARY** Read aloud these words from Listening 2. Check (✓) the ones you know. Use a dictionary to define any new or unknown words. Then discuss with a partner how the words will relate to the unit.

develop *(v.)* 🔑	**lack** *(v.)* 🔑	**top** *(adj.)* 🔑
emphasize *(v.)* 🔑	**permit** *(v.)* 🔑	**turn down** *(phr. v.)*
fear *(v.)* 🔑	**preparation** *(n.)* 🔑	

🔑 Oxford 3000™ words

iQ ONLINE **C.** Go online to listen and practice your pronunciation.

WORK WITH THE LISTENING

A. **LISTEN AND TAKE NOTES** Listen to Carl's speech. Complete the two main points he makes. Then complete the examples he gives to support his opinion.

1. **Main point 1:** We shouldn't be _____ of failure. We can

   _____ from our mistakes.

Akio Morita

2. **Main point 2:** Don't let failure _____ you. Never give up!

Examples of people who failed but went on to succeed	
Stephen King	_____ publishers turned down his first book
Michael Jordan	_____ from his high school basketball team
John Grisham	his first book, *A* _____ *to Kill*, was a failure
Akio Morita	first product was a _____ that didn't work
Thomas Edison	struggled to make the first _____ work

B. Listen to the speech again. Match the people with the statements about them.

___ 1. Stephen King   a. threw his first book in the trash

___ 2. Michael Jordan   b. failed thousands of times before succeeding

___ 3. John Grisham   c. lost a lot of money at first

___ 4. Akio Morita   d. was rejected by 16 agents and publishers

___ 5. Thomas Edison   e. "lacked skill"

C. Check (✓) the main ideas of the speech.

___ 1. Some people prefer to fail rather than succeed.

___ 2. It is sometimes necessary to fail in order to succeed.

___ 3. Modern society doesn't accept failure.

___ 4. We can learn from our failures.

___ 5. Many successful people begin by failing.

D. Complete the summary.

Carl Simmons' view is that failure is something we all

_____, but in fact it is an important stage on the road

to _____. He says we can learn a lot more from our

failures than we can from our successes. Failure is something to be

_____ by. It is a good _____ for life. We need

to experience failure, and _____ from it, in order to succeed.

E. Go online to listen to *The Advantages of Business Failure* and check your comprehension.

F. VOCABULARY Use the new vocabulary from Listening 2. Circle the answer that best matches the meaning of each word or phrase in bold.

Tip for Success

Making lists of words with similar meanings, or *synonyms*, is a good way to expand your vocabulary. Use a dictionary to study differences in meaning.

1. **develop** *(v.)*   future   changing   improve

2. **emphasize** *(v.)*   successful   importance   stress

3. **fear** *(v.)*   scare   frightening   be afraid

4. **lack** *(v.)*   missing   absence   need

5. **permit** *(v.)*   allow   helpful   ability

6. **preparation** *(n.)*   ready   training   educate

7. **top** *(adj.)*   leading   famously   seriousness

8. **turn down** *(phr. v.)* unhelpful   acceptance   refuse

iQ ONLINE **G.** Go online for more practice with the vocabulary.

SAY WHAT YOU THINK

A. Discuss the questions in a group.

1. Of the people in Listening 2, who do you think overcame the biggest difficulties? Who learned the most from their failures?

2. Give an example of a time when you succeeded after failing at first. What did you learn from your mistakes?

B. Think about the unit video, Listening 1, and Listening 2 as you discuss the questions.

1. Do you think the examples in Carl Simmons' speech support the professor's ideas about success in Listening 1? Why or why not?

2. In what ways, if any, has your view of success and failure changed?

Prefixes are added to the beginning of words to change their meaning. Understanding prefixes can help you expand your vocabulary and figure out the meaning of unknown words.

Notice the use of prefixes in these examples from Listening 2.

> Being successful is not about being a **multi**millionaire.
> (**multi**- + millionaire = multimillionaire)
> Chasing an **im**possible dream, one that you can never reach, is a frustrating waste of time and energy. (**im**- + possible = impossible)

Many prefixes give the opposite meaning to words.

> **dis**- **dis**agree
> **im**- (before words beginning with *m/p*) **im**polite
> **ir**- (before words beginning with *r*) **ir**rational

These prefixes give other meanings to words.

> **co**- (together) **co**operate
> **re**- (again) **re**place, **re**write
> **multi**- (many) **multi**purpose
> **anti**- (against) **anti**war

A. Add a prefix from the Vocabulary Skill box to complete each word.

1. _re_ view
2. ___ responsible
3. ___ like
4. ___ worker
5. ___ perfect
6. ___ social
7. ___ national
8. ___ honest
9. ___ patient
10. ___ regular
11. ___ apply
12. ___ media

B. Choose three words from Activity A. Write a sentence using each word.

1. _____

2. _____

3. _____

C. Read your sentences to a partner. Write any words you hear from Activity A in your notebook. Underline the prefixes.

iQ ONLINE **D.** Go online for more practice with prefixes.

SPEAKING

At the end of this unit, you will take part in a discussion about success and failure. Make sure to ask for and give clarification as you discuss the topic.

Grammar Simple past and present perfect

Use the **simple past** for actions that began and ended in the past. For actions that began in the past and continue up to the present, use the **present perfect**.

Simple past

Michael Jordan **played** basketball.
(He no longer plays basketball.)

Present perfect

John Grisham **has written** thirty novels.
(He is still writing novels.)

Use the simple past for actions that occurred at a specific time in the past. If the time an action occurred is not known or not important, use the present perfect.

Simple past

Stephen King **published** his first book in 1974.

Present perfect

Stephen King **has published** many books.
(When he published the books is not important.)

Use the present perfect for actions that happened more than once in the past when the focus is on how often the actions happened rather than when they happened.

Carl Simmons fails sometimes. He **has learned** from his mistakes.

Time expressions used with the simple past and present perfect

Last, *ago*, *in*, and *on* are commonly used with the simple past to show that an action was completed in the past.

For and *since* are commonly used with the present perfect to show that an action is connected to the present.

Sara started college **two years ago**.
She has been a student **for two years**.

A. Circle the correct verb forms to complete the conversation. Then practice the conversation with a partner.

Ashley: Hey, Kevin. Great shot! You know, you're a pretty good tennis player.

(<u>Did you ever enter / Have you ever entered</u>) any tennis competitions?
1

Kevin: Yes, I (<u>did / have</u>). Actually, I (<u>came / have come</u>) in second in the
      2   3

Senior Tournament at our club last year.

Ashley: Really? That's great. (<u>Did you enjoy / Have you enjoyed</u>) it?
                                                4

Kevin: Sure! Especially because it (<u>was / has been</u>) my first attempt. How
                                        5

about you?

Ashley: Oh, I play in a small local league, but I (<u>didn't win / haven't won</u>) any
                                                        6

competitions or anything. I just play for fun, to keep fit and healthy.

B. Think of a hobby or sport that you enjoy. Note your answers to these questions. Then ask and answer the questions with a partner.

1. What hobby or sport do you enjoy? _____

2. How long have you done it? _____

3. Why do you like it? _____

4. Have you ever entered any competitions? _____

5. In what ways are you "successful" at your hobby or sport?

_____

C. Complete each statement with your own ideas. Then compare sentences with a partner.

1. I _____ lately.

2. I _____ since last week.

3. I _____ yet.

4. I _____ a few years ago.

5. I _____ yesterday.

D. Go online for more practice with simple past and present perfect.

E. Go online for the grammar expansion.

Varying intonation to maintain interest

You can help your listeners follow what you are saying more easily, and also help to keep them interested while you are speaking, by varying your intonation—making your voice rise and fall—a little more than usual.

Listen to this sentence from Carl Simmons's speech. You will hear it twice. Notice how the speaker sounds more interested the second time, and this makes it more interesting and easier to follow.

☐ Just as success is something we all want, failure is something that we all fear.

Listen to some more examples. Notice how the speaker varies her intonation to make what she says easier to follow and sound more interesting.

You can learn more from your failures than you can from your successes.

Success for my grandfather is getting out of bed in the morning!

Failing is a good preparation for life.

A. Listen twice to each sentence. Which sounds more interested, Speaker 1 or Speaker 2?

	Speaker 1	Speaker 2
1. Failure is an important stage on the road to success.	☐	☐
2. We shouldn't be afraid of failure because we can learn from it.	☐	☐
3. Failure is something to be encouraged by.	☐	☐
4. Don't give up too easily!	☐	☐

B. Listen again. Repeat the sentences, using the same intonation you hear.

C. Read the paragraph below. Think about how you can use intonation to make this sound interesting and easier for listeners to follow. With a partner, take turns reading the paragraph aloud.

You need to experience failure and learn from it, in order to really succeed. Failing is a good preparation for life. It makes you stronger and more able to overcome life's problems. Don't be scared of failure! It might sound strange, but letting go of your fear of failure might help you to succeed.

D. Listen and check your answers to Activity C. Then listen and repeat, using the same intonation.

 **E.** Go online for more practice varying intonation to maintain interest.

After you listen to a speech or presentation, you can ask questions if you need **clarification** or more information about something the speaker said. Asking questions shows that you are interested and have been paying attention.

Asking for clarification

Sorry, I don't get what you mean.
What do you mean exactly?
Could you say a bit more about …?
Can you give an example?

After giving a speech or presentation, it is a good idea to ask the audience for questions. This gives you an opportunity to clarify your most important points and make sure your audience understood them.

Giving clarification

What I'm trying to say …
To give you an example …
I mean …

 A. Listen to the excerpts from a discussion. Complete the excerpts wth the phrases you hear. Then practice the conversations with a partner.

1. **Professor:** So you need to make sure the success you're aiming for is achievable.

   Student 1: _____.
   ₁

   Professor: What _____ be realistic with the goals
   ₂

   you set for yourself.

2. **Professor:** Success in one area can bring problems in others.

   Student 2: _____?
   ₃

   Professor: Well, _____, someone can be at the
   ₄
   top of her career, but her family life might be in crisis as a result.

3. **Professor:** Keep your desire for success in proportion.

   Student 3: _____?
   ₅

   Professor: Yes. I mean don't let your desire for success become greater
   than other important areas in your life.

4. **Professor:** Our definition of success alters with age.

   Student 1: _____?
   ₆

   Professor: Sure. Someone of 20 might view success as being rich, but at 50
   that same person might think of success as a happy family life.

B. Work with a partner. Take turns reading the statements from Listening 1
   and Listening 2 aloud and asking for and giving clarification.

1. Failure is an important stage on the road to success.

   A: Sorry, I don't get what you mean.
   B: What I mean by that is we learn from our mistakes.

2. If at first you don't succeed, try, try again.

3. Success for my grandfather is simply getting out of bed in the morning.

4. Failing is a good preparation for life.

iQ ONLINE **C.** Go online for more practice asking for and giving clarification.

 | Listening and Speaking   **191**

When discussing a topic, you may want to give examples to help support your opinion. Taking notes with examples is therefore a very useful skill. It allows you to organize your ideas and support your opinions in a way that is easy to refer to when you are speaking.

Look at these main points and examples from Listening 1. Notice how the main points are noted separately, next to the supporting examples.

Main points	Examples
1. Make sure your goals are realistic.	short, 30-year-old male smoker shouldn't quit job to become basketball player
2. Aiming for success should not cause stress or anxiety.	no example
3. Success can bring problems.	• famous people (TV presenters and sports stars, etc.) who have relationship problems • a high school friend, successful businessman but is now divorced

A. Think of different examples to support each main point in the chart below. Then discuss the topic of success with a partner.

Main points	Examples
1. Make sure your goals are realistic.	
2. Aiming for success should not cause stress or anxiety.	
3. Success can bring problems.	

iQ ONLINE   **B.** Go online for more practice taking notes with examples.

UNIT OBJECTIVE ▶▶▶

In this assignment, you are going to take part in a discussion about success and failure. As you prepare for the discussion, think about the Unit Question, "What can we learn from success and failure?" Use information from Listening 1, Listening 2, the unit video, and your work in this unit to support your discussion. Refer to the Self-Assessment checklist on page 196.

CONSIDER THE IDEAS

Work with a partner. Read the quotes about success and failure. Decide what the quotes mean, and think of an example for each one. Take notes in the charts.

Critical Thinking Tip

This activity asks you to **paraphrase**. **Paraphrasing**, or saying the information in your own words, helps you to understand and remember ideas better.

> "Success is not the key to happiness. Happiness is the key to success. If you love what you are doing, you will be successful."
>
> —*Albert Schweitzer*

Meaning	Example

Do you agree or disagree with this quote? Explain.

_____

_____

> "Success is never final. Failure is never fatal. Courage is what counts."
>
> —*Winston Churchill*

Meaning	Example

Do you agree or disagree with this quote? Explain.

_____

_____

> "Many of life's failures are people who did not realize how close they were to success when they gave up."
>
> —*Thomas Edison*

Meaning	Example

Do you agree or disagree with this quote? Explain.

_____

_____

PREPARE AND SPEAK

A. GATHER IDEAS **Think about what success means to you. Complete the activities.**

1. Make a list of things you have been successful at. They can be big things, such as graduating from high school, or small things, such as cooking a delicious meal.

   _____

   _____

   _____

2. Now make a list of things you have tried, but were not successful at. Again, they can be big things, such as applying for a job, or small things, such as playing a game of tennis.

   _____

   _____

   _____

B. ORGANIZE IDEAS Choose one example from each list in Activity A. Complete the outline to help you prepare to discuss your ideas.

1. **Something I was successful at:** _____

What were some of the difficulties you experienced?

_____

_____

How has this experience affected your life?

_____

_____

What have you learned from this experience?

_____

_____

_____

2. **Something I was not successful at:** _____

What were some of the difficulties you experienced?

_____

_____

How has this experience affected your life?

_____

_____

What have you learned from this experience?

_____

_____

_____

C. SPEAK **Complete these steps. Refer to the Self-Assessment checklist below before you begin.**

1. Work with a partner. Take turns telling each other about your experiences.

2. Discuss which experience you learned more from. Do not read directly from your outline. Just use it to help you remember your ideas. Use phrases from the Speaking Skill box on page 190 to ask for and give clarification.

iQ ONLINE **Go online for your alternate Unit Assignment.**

CHECK AND REFLECT

A. CHECK **Think about the Unit Assignment as you complete the Self-Assessment checklist.**

SELF-ASSESSMENT		
Yes	No	
☐	☐	I was able to speak easily about the topic.
☐	☐	My partner understood me.
☐	☐	I used vocabulary from the unit.
☐	☐	I used simple past and present perfect.
☐	☐	I varied my intonation to maintain interest.
☐	☐	I asked for and gave clarification.

B. REFLECT **Go to the Online Discussion Board to discuss these questions.**

1. What is something new you learned in this unit?

2. Look back at the Unit Question—What can we learn from success and failure? Is your answer different now than when you started this unit? If yes, how is it different? Why?

TRACK YOUR SUCCESS

Circle the words and phrases you have learned in this unit.

Nouns
determination 🔑
downside
goal 🔑 AWL
preparation 🔑
status 🔑 AWL

Verbs
achieve 🔑 AWL
develop 🔑
emphasize 🔑 AWL
fear 🔑
lack 🔑
measure 🔑
permit 🔑
ruin 🔑

Adjectives
frustrating
realistic 🔑
top 🔑

Phrasal Verbs
give up
turn down

Phrases
Can you give an example?
Could you say a bit more about …?
For example,
For instance,

Sorry, I don't get what you mean.
such as
Take, for example,
To give (you) an example,
To illustrate this,
What do you mean by …?
What I'm trying to say is …
What I mean by that is …

🔑 Oxford 3000™ words
AWL Academic Word List

Check (✓) the skills you learned. If you need more work on a skill, refer to the page(s) in parentheses.

LISTENING ☐	I can listen for examples. (p. 180)
VOCABULARY ☐	I can use prefixes. (p. 186)
GRAMMAR ☐	I can use simple past and present perfect. (p. 187)
PRONUNCIATION ☐	I can vary intonation to maintain interest. (p. 189)
SPEAKING ☐	I can ask for and give clarification. (p. 190)
NOTE TAKING ☐	I can take notes with examples. (p. 192)
UNIT OBJECTIVE ▶▶▶▶ ☐	I can gather information and ideas to discuss successful and unsuccessful personal experiences and explain what I learned from them.

AUDIO TRACK LIST

Audio can be found in the *iQ Online* Media Center. Go to <u>iQOnlinePractice.com</u>. Click on the Media Center 🎧 Choose to stream or download ⬇ the audio file you select. Not all audio files are available for download.

Page	Track Name: Q2e_03_LS_
2	U01_Q_Classroom.mp3
7	U01_Listening1_ActivityA.mp3
8	U01_Listening1_ActivityD.mp3
11	U01_ListeningSkill_Example.mp3
11	U01_ListeningSkill_ActivityA.mp3
11	U01_ListeningSkill_ActivityC.mp3
12	U01_Listening2_ActivityA.mp3
13	U01_Listening2_ActivityD.mp3
21	U01_Pronunciation_Examples.mp3
21	U01_Pronunciation_ActivityA.mp3
22	U01_SpeakingSkill_Examples.mp3
27	U02_Q_Classroom.mp3
30	U02_Listening1_ActivityA.mp3
30	U02_Listening1_ActivityB.mp3
33	U02_ListeningSkill_Examples.mp3
34	U02_ListeningSkill_ActivityA.mp3
34	U02_ListeningSkill_ActivityB.mp3
37	U02_Listening2_ActivityA.mp3
38	U02_Listening2_ActivityB.mp3
38	U02_Listening2_ActivityC.mp3
45	U02_Pronunciation_Examples.mp3
45	U02_Pronunciation_ActivityA.mp3
45	U02_Pronunciation_ActivityB.mp3
46	U02_SpeakingSkill_Examples.mp3
52	U03_Q_Classroom.mp3
57	U03_Listening1_ActivityA.mp3
57	U03_Listening1_ActivityB.mp3
57	U03_Listening1_ActivityC.mp3
60	U03_ListeningSkill_ActivityA.mp3
61	U03_Listening2_ActivityA.mp3
61	U03_Listening2_ActivityB.mp3
62	U03_Listening2_ActivityC.mp3
70	U03_Pronunciation_Examples.mp3
70	U03_Pronunciation_ActivityA.mp3
70	U03_Pronunciation_ActivityB.mp3
70	U03_Pronunciation_ActivityC.mp3
71	U03_SpeakingSkill_Examples.mp3
71	U03_SpeakingSkill_ActivityA.mp3
77	U04_Q_Classroom.mp3
79	U04_Listening1_ActivityA.mp3
80	U04_Listening1_ActivityB.mp3
82	U04_ListeningSkill_ActivityA.mp3
83	U04_ListeningSkill_ActivityB.mp3
84	U04_Listening2_ActivityA.mp3
85	U04_Listening2_ActivityC.mp3
90	U04_Grammar_ActivityA.mp3

Page	Track Name: Q2e_03_LS_
91	U04_Pronunciation_Part1_Examples.mp3
92	U04_Pronunciation_Part1_ActivityA.mp3
92	U04_Pronunciation_Part1_ActivityB.mp3
92	U04_Pronunciation_Part2_Examples.mp3
92	U04_Pronunciation_Part2_ActivityC.mp3
93	U04_Pronunciation_Part2_ActivityD.mp3
94	U04_SpeakingSkill_ActivityA.mp3
100	U05_Q_Classroom.mp3
105	U05_Listening1_ActivityA.mp3
107	U05_Listening1_ActivityD.mp3
109	U05_ListeningSkill_Part1_Example1.mp3
109	U05_ListeningSkill_Part1_Example2.mp3
109	U05_ListeningSkill_Part1_Example3.mp3
110	U05_ListeningSkill_Part1_ActivityA.mp3
110	U05_ListeningSkill_Part2_Examples.mp3
111	U05_ListeningSkill_Part2_ActivityC.mp3
111	U05_ListeningSkill_Part2_ActivityD.mp3
112	U05_Listening2_ActivityA.mp3
112	U05_Listening2_ActivityD.mp3
119	U05_Pronunciation_Examples.mp3
119	U05_Pronunciation_ActivityA.mp3
120	U05_Pronunciation_ActivityB.mp3
121	U05_SpeakingSkill_ActivityA.mp3
122	U05_UnitAssignment.mp3
127	U06_Q_Classroom.mp3
130	U06_Listening1_ActivityA.mp3
131	U06_Listening1_ActivityC.mp3
133	U06_ListeningSkill_Examples.mp3
133	U06_ListeningSkill_ActivityA.mp3
133	U06_ListeningSkill_ActivityB.mp3
134	U06_Listening2_ActivityA.mp3
135	U06_Listening2_ActivityC.mp3
141	U06_Pronunciation_Examples.mp3
141	U06_Pronunciation_ActivityA.mp3
141	U06_Pronunciation_ActivityB.mp3
141	U06_Pronunciation_ActivityC.mp3
141	U06_Pronunciation_ActivityD.mp3
143	U06_SpeakingSkill_ActivityA.mp3
145	U06_NoteTakingSkill_ActivityC.mp3
150	U07_Q_Classroom.mp3
153	U07_Listening1_ActivityA.mp3
154	U07_Listening1_ActivityC.mp3
157	U07_ListeningSkill_Examples.mp3
158	U07_ListeningSkill_ActivityA.mp3
160	U07_Listening2_ActivityA.mp3
161	U07_Listening2_ActivityB.mp3

Page	Track Name: Q2e_03_LS_
167	U07_Pronunciation_ActivityA.mp3
168	U07_Pronunciation_ActivityB.mp3
168	U07_SpeakingSkill_ActivityA.mp3
175	U08_Q_Classroom.mp3
178	U08_Listening1_ActivityA.mp3
178	U08_Listening1_ActivityC.mp3
181	U08_ListeningSkill_ActivityA.mp3
181	U08_ListeningSkill_ActivityB.mp3
183	U08_Listening2_ActivityA.mp3
184	U08_Listening2_ActivityB.mp3
189	U08_Pronunciation_Example1.mp3
189	U08_Pronunciation_Example2.mp3
189	U08_Pronunciation_ActivityA.mp3
189	U08_Pronunciation_ActivityB.mp3
190	U08_Pronunciation_ActivityD.mp3
190	U08_SpeakingSkill_ActivityA.mp3

AUTHORS AND CONSULTANTS

Authors

Miles Craven has worked in English language education since 1988, teaching in private language schools, British Council centers, and universities in Italy, Portugal, Spain, Hong Kong, Japan, and the U.K. He has a wide range of experience as a teacher, teacher trainer, examiner, course designer, and textbook writer. Miles is author or co-author of over 30 textbooks, and regularly presents at conferences around the world. He also acts as Advisor for Executive Education programs at the Møller Centre for Continuing Education Ltd., Churchill College, University of Cambridge. His research focuses on helping students develop the skills and strategies they need to become confident communicators. He currently specializes in exam preparation for the TOEIC test.

Kristin Donnalley Sherman holds an M. Ed. in TESL from the University of North Carolina, Charlotte. She has taught ESL/EFL at Central Piedmont Community College in Charlotte, North Carolina for more than fifteen years, and has taught a variety of subjects, including grammar, reading, composition, listening, and speaking. She has written student books, teacher's editions, and workbooks in the area of academic ESL/EFL. In addition, she regularly presents at conferences and workshops internationally.

Series Consultants

ONLINE INTEGRATION

Chantal Hemmi holds an Ed.D. TEFL and is a Japan-based teacher trainer and curriculum designer. Since leaving her position as Academic Director of the British Council in Tokyo, she has been teaching at the Center for Language Education and Research at Sophia University on an EAP/CLIL program offered for undergraduates. She delivers lectures and teacher trainings throughout Japan, Indonesia, and Malaysia.

COMMUNICATIVE GRAMMAR

Nancy Schoenfeld holds an M.A. in TESOL from Biola University in La Mirada, California, and has been an English language instructor since 2000. She has taught ESL in California and Hawaii, and EFL in Thailand and Kuwait. She has also trained teachers in the United States and Indonesia. Her interests include teaching vocabulary, extensive reading, and student motivation. She is currently an English Language Instructor at Kuwait University.

WRITING

Marguerite Ann Snow holds a Ph.D. in Applied Linguistics from UCLA. She teaches in the TESOL M.A. program in the Charter College of Education at California State University, Los Angeles. She was a Fulbright scholar in Hong Kong and Cyprus. In 2006, she received the President's Distinguished Professor award at Cal State, LA. She has trained EFL teachers in Algeria, Argentina, Brazil, Egypt, Libya, Morocco, Pakistan, Peru, Spain, and Turkey. She is the author/editor of publications in the areas of integrated content, English for academic purposes, and standards for English teaching and learning. She recently served as a co-editor of *Teaching English as a Second or Foreign Language* (4th ed.).

VOCABULARY

Cheryl Boyd Zimmerman is a Professor at California State University, Fullerton. She specializes in second-language vocabulary acquisition, an area in which she is widely published. She teaches graduate courses on second-language acquisition, culture, vocabulary, and the fundamentals of TESOL and is a frequent invited speaker on topics related to vocabulary teaching and learning. She is the author of *Word Knowledge: A Vocabulary Teacher's Handbook* and Series Director of *Inside Reading, Inside Writing,* and *Inside Listening and Speaking,* all published by Oxford University Press.

ASSESSMENT

Lawrence J. Zwier holds an M.A. in TESL from the University of Minnesota. He is currently the Associate Director for Curriculum Development at the English Language Center at Michigan State University in East Lansing. He has taught ESL/EFL in the United States, Saudi Arabia, Malaysia, Japan, and Singapore.

iQ ONLINE extends your learning beyond the classroom. This online content is specifically designed for you! *iQ Online* gives you flexible access to essential content.

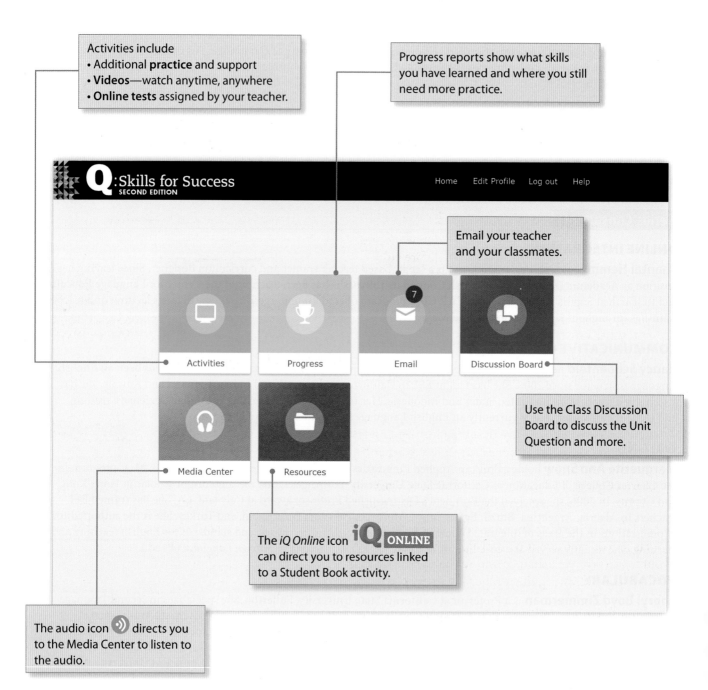

Activities include
• Additional **practice** and support
• **Videos**—watch anytime, anywhere
• **Online tests** assigned by your teacher.

Progress reports show what skills you have learned and where you still need more practice.

Email your teacher and your classmates.

Activities

Progress

Email

Discussion Board

Use the Class Discussion Board to discuss the Unit Question and more.

Media Center

Resources

The *iQ Online* icon **iQ ONLINE** can direct you to resources linked to a Student Book activity.

The audio icon directs you to the Media Center to listen to the audio.

SEE THE INSIDE FRONT COVER FOR HOW TO REGISTER FOR *iQ ONLINE* FOR THE FIRST TIME.

Take Control of Your Learning

You have the choice of where and how you complete the activities. Access your activities and view your progress at any time.

Your teacher may

- assign *iQ Online* as homework,
- do the activities with you in class, or
- let you complete the activities at a pace that is right for you.

iQ Online makes it easy to access everything you need.

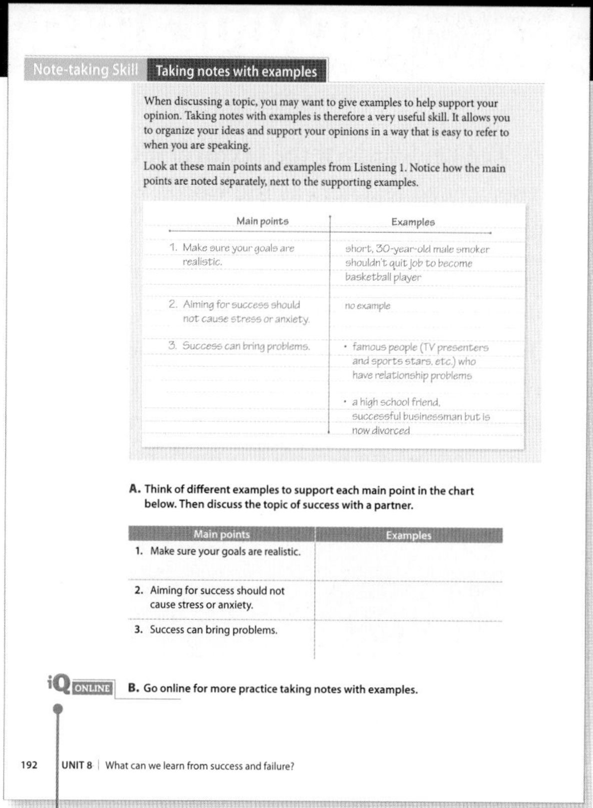

Set Clear Goals

STEP 1 If it is your first time, look through the site. See what learning opportunities are available.

STEP 2 The Student Book provides the framework and purpose for each online activity. Before going online, notice the goal of the exercises you are going to do.

STEP 3 Stay on top of your work, following the teacher's instructions.

STEP 4 Use *iQ Online* for review. You can use the materials any time. It is easy for you to do follow-up activities when you have missed a class or want to review.

Manage Your Progress

The activities in *iQ Online* are designed for you to work independently. You can become a confident learner by monitoring your progress and reviewing the activities at your own pace. You may already be used to working online, but if you are not, go to your teacher for guidance.

Check 'View Reports' to monitor your progress. The reports let you track your own progress at a glance. Think about your own performance and set new goals that are right for you, following the teacher's instructions.

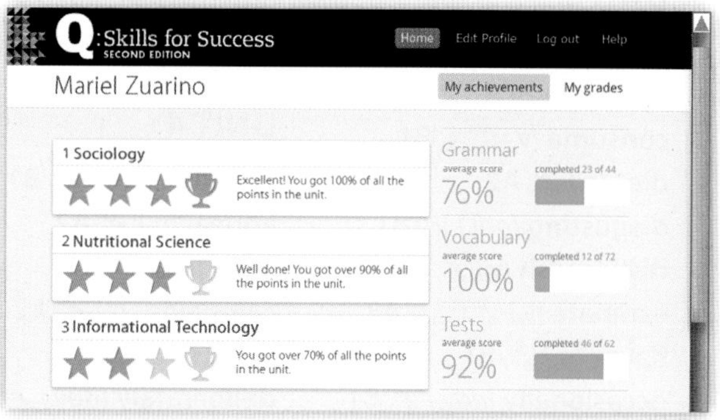

iQ Online is a research-based solution specifically designed for English language learners that extends learning beyond the classroom. I hope these steps help you make the most of this essential content.

Chantal Hemmi, EdD TEFL
Center for Language Education and Research
Sophia University, Japan

Sidebar (right column)

When discussing a topic, you may want to give examples to help support your opinion. Taking notes with examples is therefore a very useful skill. It allows you to organize your ideas and support your opinions in a way that is easy to refer to when you are speaking.

Look at these main points and examples from Listening 1. Notice how the main points are noted separately, next to the supporting examples.

Main points	Examples
1. Make sure your goals are realistic.	short, 30-year-old male smoker shouldn't quit job to become basketball player
2. Aiming for success should not cause stress or anxiety.	no example
3. Success can bring problems.	• famous people (TV presenters and sports stars, etc.) who have relationship problems • a high school friend, successful businessman but is now divorced

A. Think of different examples to support each main point in the chart below. Then discuss the topic of success with a partner.

Main points	Examples
1. Make sure your goals are realistic.	
2. Aiming for success should not cause stress or anxiety.	
3. Success can bring problems.	

iQ ONLINE **B.** Go online for more practice taking notes with examples.

Notice the icon. It directs you to the online materials linked to the Student Book activities.

Q:Skills for Success SECOND EDITION — Home · Edit Profile · Log out · Help

Mariel Zuarino — My achievements · My grades

1 Sociology ★★★🏆 Excellent! You got 100% of all the points in the unit.

Grammar average score 76% completed 23 of 44

2 Nutritional Science ★★★🏆 Well done! You got over 90% of all the points in the unit.

Vocabulary average score 100% completed 12 of 72

3 Informational Technology ★★★🏆 You got over 70% of all the points in the unit.

Tests average score 92% completed 46 of 62

🔑 The keywords of the **Oxford 3000**™ have been carefully selected by a group of language experts and experienced teachers as the words which should receive priority in vocabulary study because of their importance and usefulness.

AWL **The Academic Word List** is the most principled and widely accepted list of academic words. Averil Coxhead gathered information from academic materials across the academic disciplines to create this word list.

The Common European Framework of Reference for Languages (CEFR) provides a basic description of what language learners have to do to use language effectively. The system contains 6 reference levels: **A1, A2, B1, B2, C1, C2.** CEFR leveling provided by the Word Family Framework, created by Richard West and published by the British Council. http://www.learnenglish.org.uk/wff/

UNIT 1

assume (v.) 🔑 AWL, A1
behavior (n.) 🔑, A1
briefly (adv.) 🔑, B1
conscious (adj.) 🔑, A2
effective (adj.) 🔑, A1
encounter (n.) 🔑 AWL, B1
error (n.) 🔑 AWL, A2
expert (n.) 🔑 AWL, A2
negative (adj.) 🔑 AWL, A2
positive (adj.) 🔑 AWL, A2
sample (n.) 🔑, A2
select (v.) 🔑 AWL, A2
suspicious (adj.) 🔑, B1

UNIT 2

complex (adj.) 🔑 AWL, A2
concentrate (v.) 🔑 AWL, A2
consume (v.) AWL, B1
diet (n.) 🔑, A2
disgusting (adj.) 🔑, B1
distinguish (v.) 🔑, B1
estimate (v.) 🔑 AWL, A2
flavor (n.) 🔑, B1
occasionally (adv.) 🔑, B1
mix (v.) 🔑, A2
mood (n.) 🔑, B1
spicy (adj.) 🔑, B1
swallow (v.) 🔑, B1
trend (n.) 🔑 AWL, A2
wise (adj.) 🔑, B1

UNIT 3

adapt (v.) 🔑 AWL, B1
considerably (adv.) 🔑, B2
cope (v.) 🔑, B1
crisis (n.) 🔑, A2
curious (adj.) 🔑, B1
handle (v.) 🔑, A2
justify (v.) 🔑 AWL, B1
permanent (adj.) 🔑, A2
position (n.) 🔑, B1
research (n.) 🔑 AWL, A2
steady (adj.) 🔑, B1
struggle (v.) 🔑, A2
suffer (v.) 🔑, A1
support (v.) 🔑, B2
unemployed (adj.) 🔑, B1
wages (n.) 🔑, A2

UNIT 4

aimed at (phr.) 🔑, B1
appeal (n.) 🔑, A2
brand (n.) 🔑, B1
campaign (n.) 🔑, A2
claim (v.) 🔑, A1
deliberately (adv.) 🔑, B1
evidence (n.) 🔑 AWL, A1
injury (n.) 🔑 AWL, A2
monitor (v.) 🔑 AWL, B1
persuade (v.) 🔑, A2
regulations (n.) 🔑 AWL, A2
relate to (phr.) 🔑, A1
withdraw (v.) 🔑, A1

UNIT 5

audience (n.) 🔑, A1
discover (v.) 🔑, A1
embarrass (v.) 🔑, B2
expose (v.) 🔑 AWL, B1
financial (adj.) 🔑 AWL, A1
funds (n.) 🔑 AWL, A1
income (n.) 🔑 AWL, A1
invention (n.) 🔑, B2
investigate (v.) 🔑 AWL, A2
locate (v.) 🔑 AWL, B1
model (n.) 🔑, A2
mystery (n.) 🔑, B1
previous (adj.) 🔑 AWL, A1
promote (v.) 🔑 AWL, B1
prove (v.) 🔑, A1
publish (v.) 🔑 AWL, A1
reputation (n.) 🔑, B1
retire (v.) 🔑, B1
solve (v.) 🔑, A2
threaten (v.) 🔑, A1

UNIT 6

appropriate (adj.) 🔑 AWL, A1
benefit (n.) 🔑 AWL, A1
consumer (n.) 🔑 AWL, A1
demand (v.) 🔑, B1
fair (adj.) 🔑, A2
guilty (adj.) 🔑, A2
ignore (v.) 🔑 AWL, A1
impact (n.) 🔑 AWL, B1
influence (v.) 🔑, A2
lie (v.) 🔑, A1

profit (n.) 🔑, A1
sensible (adj.) 🔑, B1
trust (v.) 🔑, A2

UNIT 7

acquire (v.) 🔑 AWL, A2
analysis (n.) 🔑 AWL, A1
associated with (adj.) 🔑, B2
circumstances (n.) 🔑 AWL, A2
complicated (adj.) 🔑, B1
conduct (v.) 🔑 AWL, A2
demonstrate (v.) 🔑 AWL, A2
dramatic (adj.) 🔑 AWL, B1
immediate (adj.) 🔑, A2
independence (n.) 🔑, A2
outcome (n.) AWL, A2
pleasure (n.) 🔑, A2
somewhat (adv.) 🔑 AWL, A2

UNIT 8

achieve (v.) 🔑 AWL, A1
determination (n.) 🔑, B1
develop (v.) 🔑, B1
emphasize (v.) 🔑 AWL, A2
fear (v.) 🔑, A2
goal (n.) 🔑 AWL, A2
lack (v.) 🔑, B1
measure (v.) 🔑, A1
permit (v.) 🔑, A2
preparation (n.) 🔑, A2
realistic (adj.) 🔑, B2
ruin (v.) 🔑, B2
status (n.) 🔑 AWL, A1
top (adj.) 🔑, A2